MULTIPLY YOUR SUCCESS WITH

FENGSHUI

MULTIPLY YOUR SUCCESS WITH

FENGSHUI

*Finding Wealth and Happiness through
Chinese Metaphysics*

VLADIMIR ZAKHAROV

Published by Advantage, Charleston, South Carolina.
Member of Advantage Media Group.

ADVANTAGE is a registered trademark and the Advantage colophon is a trademark of Advantage Media Group, Inc.

Printed in the United States of America.

ISBN: 978-1-59932-484-5
LCCN: 2015956699

This publication is designed to provide accurate and authoritative information in regard to the subject matter covered. It is sold with the understanding that the publisher is not engaged in rendering legal, accounting, or other professional services. If legal advice or other expert assistance is required, the services of a competent professional person should be sought.

Advantage Media Group is proud to be a part of the Tree Neutral® program. Tree Neutral offsets the number of trees consumed in the production and printing of this book by taking proactive steps such as planting trees in direct proportion to the number of trees used to print books. To learn more about Tree Neutral, please visit www.treeneutral.com. To learn more about Advantage's commitment to being a responsible steward of the environment, please visit www.advantagefamily.com/green

Advantage Media Group is a publisher of business, self-improvement, and professional development books and online learning. We help entrepreneurs, business leaders, and professionals share their Stories, Passion, and Knowledge to help others Learn & Grow. Do you have a manuscript or book idea that you would like us to consider for publishing? Please visit advantagefamily.com or call 1.866.775.1696.

TABLE OF CONTENTS

NO BS FENG SHUI: SO MUCH MORE THAN FROGS AND COINS

I'm often asked how I came to the practice and teaching of Feng Shui. Actually, I began as a student of Western astrology in the early 1990s, becoming a professional consultant in the former Soviet Union, but found that the demand for those kinds of services just didn't match my needs as a practitioner. I've never been the employee type; I think I have worked two entire weeks for someone else in my life. I've sold things on the streets; I've lived hand to mouth. What held it together for me even in the darkest times were my Buddhist practices, which had also been with me since the '90s. While being unemployed gave me plenty of time to practice my meditation, I knew I needed to find meaningful work that resonated with my values, something that aligned with my interest in spiritual seeking, and most importantly, something that could help people on both the practical and spiritual levels.

Around that time, I came across a couple of books about Feng Shui and bought them out of curiosity. It wasn't very broadly known of in that part of the world at that time, and I found the whole concept intriguing. A Buddhist friend from Germany saw those books on my coffee table and expressed surprise that I was just getting into it, because the practice of Feng Shui had been popular for some time in Germany. She drew a floor plan of my apartment and brought a Feng Shui master over to see it. He gave me some advice, for instance, to take my bed and move it to another room and to place a water fountain in a certain spot. The advice he gave was all easy to accomplish, so I implemented his suggestions, figuring I had nothing to lose.

I wasn't sure what to expect—but within two months, I went from being broke to being the co-owner of two small businesses: a translation agency and a small printing company. It seemed nothing short of miraculous, going from being completely jobless for a few years to being co-owner of two businesses in just two months! I was surprised, to put it mildly. At one point in my youth, my financial situation had been so bad that I had lived at the train station and even a couple of times had stolen bread to survive, so I knew what poverty was, and I had no desire to return to it. Now I had an actual income—a small one, but I was a director of a company with my own office and employees. Unbelievable!

You can probably understand why this experience gave me a burning interest in getting to know more about Feng Shui. Back in the late 1990s, I connected with a friend of mine, Anatoly Sokolov, who was practicing Feng Shui, and I brought him to Kiev to conduct a seminar for my mates. Later, I attended a seminar presented by German Feng Shui master **Lothar Baier**, who was also a Buddhist. We became drinking buddies during that four-day seminar, and somehow every night I wound up with him and two ladies at the nearest bar. I got the most interesting lessons from him as we chatted at that bar; he shared some private stories and secret formulas that he didn't teach during the seminar—it was a great time.

I went to Malaysia to attend a Feng Shui seminar with a well-known teacher and writer, Joey Yap, a terrific instructor and a continuing source of inspiration for me. But after the class and my hotel room were paid for, I was down to my last $500. Talk about putting your money where your mouth is; I had literally put everything I had on the table of Feng Shui knowledge. If I couldn't make it work for me, I had no idea how I'd earn a living. Fortunately, it did work! So I continued my live events and consulting activity.

During that class in Kuala Lumpur I also made some great connections, including the generous and very deep Feng Shui Master Vin Leo from Singapore, who became my friend and continued to share his amazing Feng Shui knowledge through the following years.

I wanted to know more, so I attended other seminars overseas in France, India, Singapore, and Malaysia. My income was good enough at that point to allow me to pay for those classes, although they were expensive. But in 2004, several things happened that shifted the course of my life yet again. First of all, the political situation changed in Ukraine, beginning with the Orange Revolution. That created a ripple effect in the economy, and as one of my businesses was reliant on government regulations, it suddenly no longer existed. At that point, I had invested a lot of time and money into learning the art of Feng Shui, so I needed to decide either to practice it professionally or to quit what was otherwise just an expensive hobby and shift to something else.

I started my Feng Shui seminar activities in 2002, and in 2004 I decided to do them full time. Because the economy was so bad in Ukraine, I started giving a few classes in Russia. My classes became popular in Moscow, and I very quickly found myself as one of the top guys in the field. I was making enough money to support my lifestyle and to allow me to continue to attend classes with Feng Shui masters overseas. Still, my earning power seemed to be limited by how many classes I could give, so the possibility of becoming wealthy didn't even occur to me.

In 2010, I decided to shift my model from live events to online classes, offering distance learning, live and recorded webinars, and so on. In terms of income, that created a huge shift, and I found myself a millionaire within a couple of years. That said, I often worked sixteen-hour days, which makes me think I'm paying the price for not having worked in my youth by now having to work twice as hard. Now I've upgraded my own Feng Shui once again, so I don't need to work as much anymore.

Part of the reason for my success, I think, is that I prefer to apply the teachings I learn to myself first and then teach them to others, because from the very beginning, this method has worked for me.

How does Feng Shui work? Not, as some people seem to think, as a money machine that will rain cash down on you as you sleep. It's kind of weird how something like bed positioning or a water fountain can change your life, but I've experienced it myself and helped many others to do the same. **Feng Shui is a multiplier**—let's say by a factor of ten—but you must have something to multiply to begin with. **Ten multiplied by zero is still zero**. If you have no business, no career, and no talent and aren't willing to make any effort, nothing can help you to succeed. Fortunately, most people are willing to work toward what they want—and Feng Shui multiplies those efforts and makes them far more fruitful.

Many people are skeptical of Chinese metaphysics, but the real problem isn't with the metaphysics itself but with people's understanding of it. What most people call Feng Shui is basically a Chinese style of interior design involving use of familiar Chinese objects to increase luck and fortune, like frogs with coins in their mouths, wind chimes, or Chinese coins to put on your computer to attract more wealth. But these kinds of things are not related to Feng Shui at all.

They're more like the kind of kitsch that Chinese village housewives decorate with.

In contrast, let's take Singapore, a place where Feng Shui is very popular and where I think you'd find that, to some degree, every bank, supermarket, small shop, or big shopping mall applies Feng Shui principles to their design. If you fly to Singapore and go to any bank or any shopping mall, you won't see any dragons or Chinese coins or frogs with coins in their mouths. Rather, you need to know some formulas and do some measurements to recognize their use of Feng Shui. There is very little probability that the establishments are set up as they are by accident. The placement of a door in a building, or a building's relationship to the road outside, doesn't happen by accident in Singapore; it's all part of the art of Feng Shui.

I once had a client whose husband confronted me and said that he thought Feng Shui was bullshit. He was surprised when I agreed with him—but I knew what he meant. He wasn't talking about real Feng Shui but about all those kitschy frogs and coins and fountains. Feng Shui is planned, practical, scientific, and provable—and you can see evidence of that everywhere you look. For instance, some buildings bring bad luck. You've probably noticed that some places always seem to be for rent; one shop owner rents the place, then in six months he's gone. Another one rents this same place, and in three months, he's gone. And the story repeats itself over and over again. Is it likely that they're all just bad businessmen? Is there really no way to explain why they'd have identical bad experiences? I think there is: bad Feng Shui.

Let me give you a few examples of some of my clients' experiences. I had a student who I showed how to use a technique to warm her wealth star in her home, which improves luck. It's called "warming" because we actually use a candle to warm a certain sector of our house. My students use this technique to make a wealth spike; something like getting a one-time gift or buying a winning lottery ticket. It's not so much about making more money, but it's about money just suddenly showing up for you. This student was standing by the window, and the window was open. A couple was quarreling in the apartment above hers. The wife of the guy was yelling, "I don't need your money!" and started throwing money out of the window. The money started falling down, and a $50 bill flew into her apartment. A couple of hundred bucks flew into the apartment below hers, which was in the same sector. Money was falling down on people walking below. Another student of mine did this technique and went out on a walk. A wallet full of money came sailing down from a building she was walking under and hit her in the head. In a third instance, after doing this technique, one friend of mine found a ring with a diamond just a few steps away from his apartment.

Do you want to try the same kind of technique by yourself and bring more wealth energy into your life? Visit my webpage and download the **free** report "How to warm up the money star and attract wealth" at: fengshuimillionaire.com/fengshuistartadeng.html.

Now obviously I'm not guaranteeing that people will get hit in a head with a wallet or stumble across a diamond ring. But in relation to things we're used to thinking of as outside of our influence—what we call "luck"—we need a more metaphysical way of thinking. Western society tells us that we're responsible for everything in our lives, but it's just not as simple as that. Quite often, people try to force open the door if it is closed. Let's say, for instance, that I decided to become a musician. There's no way it could work, because I have no talent and no ear for music. But people want to believe they can go in whatever direction they choose in their lives, regardless of their limitations. They're sold on this idea by motivational speakers, who tell them that they can have whatever they want if they simply believe in themselves. That's a seductive message, but I think it's total BS.

Feng Shui is a part of the larger picture of Chinese metaphysics. Another important piece of Chinese metaphysics is Chinese astrology, which concerns our qualities, our strengths, and our weaknesses. Chinese metaphysics is a clever way to check your strengths and weaknesses—in other words, which doors can be opened by you and which cannot—and helps you to see the way to go. When you decide which path, which direction to follow in life (which actually can be done by Chinese astrology), then you can apply Feng Shui to let your house support your goals. In the process of making this application, variables such as the placement and direction of your bed, oven, and table can make a huge difference in your life. There are energy channels in your house, and those channels can be activated. There's a certain way that energy channels can be activated in your body by acupuncture or by a doctor. These channels need to be activated at certain calculated times to have a very predictable result on your love, health, and well-being. Rich people live in rich places, and poor people live in poor places. Your house makes a difference. Your surroundings make a difference. Your dwelling place has a certain wealth capacity, health capacity, or relationship capacity. The easiest way to visualize this idea is to look at a small cup; what will happen if you try to pour a lot of water into it? It won't hold all of the water, because it hasn't got the capacity. The same holds true for our endeavors and their relationship to where we are. At certain moments of our life we have greater capacity than at other moments.

Chinese metaphysics and Feng Shui can help us identify and change those things in our surroundings that are holding us back, open the closed doors, and take us from want to prosperity in all areas of our lives, from relationships to wealth. If you're a seeker who's ready to explore a new way of thinking, let's dig into what Feng Shui is and what it can do.

CHAPTER ONE:

The "Language" of Feng Shui

What is Feng Shui? In the simplest terms, Feng Shui is a kind of language that explains to us why certain things happen and how we can stimulate unseen, yet powerful, forces to produce a desired outcome. As I noted in the first section, in terms of Feng Shui, good places attract certain kinds of people, and those people prosper in those places. Bad places attract certain kinds of people, and those people suffer in those places. Feng Shui is just a language to help us to understand and explain why some places are good and other places are bad. The ideas are not unlike those behind Neuro-Linguistic Programming, which provides a way to explain how people communicate with each other, what ways are effective, and which ways are not effective.

For example, everyone recognizes that certain areas in our cities are better, more desirable, than others. Feng Shui just tries to bring such areas into our awareness, so we can determine what's good, or what is not good, about such areas. Otherwise, we are just caught up by our tendencies to do as we've always done, which may mean that we're drawn by our destiny to live in poorer areas and suffer poverty and loneliness. That doesn't have to be the case. By training our consciousness, we can shift our behavior and, by doing so, make huge changes in our circumstances. That might be as simple as changing where we live, by not renting a "bad" apartment. That might mean that we pay more, although that isn't always the case. The important thing is that it puts us into a whole different area, and sometimes that small shift is powerful enough to change everything about our lives.

QI AND ENERGY CHANNELS

I hear a lot of people talking about the concept of *qi* (sometimes written as *chi*) without having a very clear understanding of what it actually is. Qi is quite frequently misinterpreted. To put it in its simplest terms, qi is a word for energy. Of course, we can simply use the word "energy," but for me, qi also includes the element of luck. When we talk about someone having good luck, it means they've got good qi, just as the idea of bad luck describes having bad qi. It's an unseen force that influences our lives. It's like currents of energy in the body. Chinese medicine and Chinese acupuncture use herbs and needles to stimulate these unseen currents of energy in our body, to help make this energy flow smoothly.

We who practice Feng Shui do the same in our offices and our apartments. We try to pick up certain important areas, certain energy points, and stimulate them by using a candle or a water fountain, by moving furniture, or whatever is called for. Additionally, we use Feng Shui to identify the most auspicious days on which to do those things in order to obtain the best possible results.

We can see the results and effects of this qi, but we cannot measure it directly. Sometimes I use the metaphor of radiation. Radiation existed for a long, long time before mankind invented the equipment to measure it. If you're in a very radioactive area, you are more likely to suffer all sorts of diseases as a consequence, and perhaps even die from them, but this radiation is unseen. You might not know what it is that is making you ill. It simply is. It's much the same with qi. If we spend a lot of time in a particular area of our apartment, for instance, we can see the effect of this positioning in that we'll suffer from diseases, broken relationships, and bankruptcy in consequence of it. It's important to note that those consequences have nothing to do with how the apartment looks; it can look quite nice. It's not a question of esthetics but of qi or the lack of it.

That's the difficulty with Feng Shui; so much of what influences our destinies is invisible. We can see the effect, but we can't see the actual cause or why it's happening. And people think they're somehow personally responsible for the bad outcomes that follow; "Something is wrong with me, that's why I was divorced," or "That's why I'm always broke." Sometimes it *is* your fault—but it's also true that very often your location has a big role in how your life unfolds. The flow of qi can influence health, energy, and relationships, even love. If a relationship is suffering, perhaps a change in qi can resolve the problems. Perhaps not 100 percent but enough to change a failing relationship into something positive.

We can talk about qi everywhere. We can talk about qi in our body, in our apartment, in our house, in our office. We can talk about qi inside of certain dates or certain years, months, days, and hours. We can talk about qi inside of our astrology chart. If you're well trained in the practice of *qigong*, the Chinese practice to manipulate energy inside of your body, you can actually feel qi itself with your arms, and you can move this qi. But the general public can't do that, so I prefer to talk about cause and effect rather than talking about direct manipulation of qi, because if you have never practiced qigong, you can't have had that experience. The practice of qigong is based on the idea that there are three centers of energy in our bodies: one in the belly at about where the navel is, one around the heart, and one inside of the head. The one below the belly button collects physical energy. The one near to the heart is about emotional energy or emotional qi. The one inside the head is about mental qi. The lowest form of the energy is the one at belly level; it's like unrefined crude oil. When it's refined, as oil is refined to gasoline, it goes up higher to the heart level, and when it's further refined, it goes even higher, to the head level. We all have this basic, physical energy. If we didn't, then there would be no way to think, because the energy wouldn't be there for our brains.

We can use this same kind of thinking for Feng Shui. It's basic energy. It has nothing to do with beliefs. It's about containing and focusing a sort of unrefined energy, energy that we can learn to refine and channel to work for us in the same way that oil can be refined to heat our home or gas can power our car.

The practice of Feng Shui talks about channeling and refining the qi of our surroundings, of our buildings or our neighborhoods. It acknowledges and works with this unseen force, rather than ignoring it. When we think we can control everything in our lives by good business planning, we're making a mistake, because we're not thinking about the surrounding environment.

Basically there are two ways of thinking in the Western world. One of these is the notion that people live within a sort of magic vault. There's a movie called *The Secret*, one that's well known and has made its producers a fortune. It talks about harnessing the Law of Attraction: how imagining the kind of life you want will create the reality. Say you'd like a sports car. If you start your brain thinking of what you would feel if you had this sports car, if you can imagine it fully and immerse yourself in this feeling, then finally you'll attract the sports car and have it in fact. It's a way of thinking that has been popularized in several different iterations over the years; I call it *magical thinking*. In most cases, as far as I'm concerned, it has missing components, e.g. it can be within the realm of possibilities and deeply in your heart that you must believe, and whatever you visualize will happen. I can ask my friend, who works a taxi driver, to imagine being an owner of a Porsche or a Ferrari ten times a day, but I'm pretty sure that no matter how hard he tries to imagine it into existence, it won't turn up in his garage. But, the opposite, purely *rational thinking* says that in order to succeed in business you need to plan everything, be trained in marketing, put a lot of effort into it, etc., and that doing those things will guarantee you'll have a successful enterprise. I can find you a million examples to prove that this way of thinking is equally wrongheaded.

There's a middle road, one followed more in the Eastern world, one that includes certain magic components, if you will; we need to be inspired, certainly, to adopt a certain way of thinking, a certain energy state, to actually achieve those well-planned and refined business goals. You can't get there without the complementary components of both kinds of thought and preparation.

It's an expression of polarity, like Yin and Yang. There's a rational way and an extrarational way, and if we bring them together, we create a complete picture that finally works to affect our circumstances.

APPLYING FENG SHUI TO LIFE

To apply that to Feng Shui, let's say that we have a certain business plan and certain mindset and a few years' training as a book-keeper, businessman, or in some profession. But if our office doesn't support us, or if we hire wrong people, we're screwed. I'm not talking in terms of their resumes; in fact, the qualities of those people, from the rational perspective, may be good. They're well trained, competent—but they just bring bad luck. **Some people, whatever they do, experience failure and bring it with them**. Others, for equally mysterious reasons, can't help but succeed. I don't know why it's true, but **when these people touch something, it becomes gold**. Anything they touch brings happiness; their ideas flower and inspire and succeed for them. But for others, the opposite is true. They try just as hard, and look just as good on paper, but they can't win for losing. Let's say you know a doctor who's a good doctor in terms of training. But if he does an operation, his patients often die on him. Why? Somehow, the vibration is wrong. Probably, he just attracts the patient who is too ill to survive anyhow, whose number is up. I contend that this all has to do with nurturing and channeling qi.

Westerners find it exotic how ancient Chinese organized their lives. Every year, a Chinese almanac is produced—millions of copies are printed. I believe that it's the most published book in all times and nations. The book focuses on every day of that specific year and talks about which day is good, which hour is good, and which is not. Every year, people buy the new almanac and plan their business and personal life around its recommendations. For them, it's not exotic; it's just how things are done and understood to work.

They analyze the energy pattern of certain stars and days. One may be called something like the "Day of Clash," when energy clashes. It's a bad idea to start new things on this day: to start your trip on this day, to get married on this day, to open your business that day, and so on. And sometimes there are funny notes, such as, "Don't do anything on this day; instead, go out and drink." I know it sounds crazy, but, yes, it's actually noted in this book that certain days are so crappy that it's more productive to lock yourself inside of the bathroom and smoke crack than to start a new business or anything else.

> You can find a **free** online version of good and bad dates on our online service at www.ba-zi.com.

How does all this work in real time? For me, the best way to explain it is to say that the world is like a hologram; each part represents everything, so whatever is happening in that moment will present the answer to your question, if you know how to pay attention and interpret it. I've seen it many times in my practice: Once a businessman client was with me in a restaurant, asking if his new venture would be successful. While he was asking me that question, a couple was quarreling nearby. This became the answer to the question. If the businessman was prepared for quarreling and lawsuits, he could go ahead; otherwise he should try a different path. This example shows how the world can be presenting you with the answer even as you're asking the question.

SYNCHRONICITY

One day I was walking on the street, deep in thought, considering a business enterprise. Should I get involved in it or not? Suddenly, a homeless man, clearly deranged, walked up to me and said plainly, "You're stupid." The Universe had answered my question. For whatever reasons, the enterprise I was weighing would not be a smart thing to get involved with.

Here's a third example that's a little embarrassing but worth sharing anyhow. Let's be honest here; sometimes we all bring our cellphones into the bathroom with us, right? It's a nice quiet place to return a call or check emails. And since nobody can see you, there's no shame in it. Well, say I was in the bathroom when I get a text; it was from someone who wanted to start a business venture with me. Let's think about it; here I was, in a literally shitty place, as I was getting this text. Guess what? The Universe was saying, "This is a shitty deal. Don't get involved." That's happened to me, and all I could think of was, "Why didn't this guy text me two minutes ago, when I was sitting by the swimming pool?" **It's synchronicity; everything is related.**

There is an art in Chinese metaphysics we call *Xuan Kong*, which can be translated to "flying stars" or "space and time." It's a mystical art that allows us to interpret certain events. In this art, we're taught we need to translate events into numbers. (I understand that the following paragraph has no meaning for you unless you are very familiar with Lo Shu, trigrams, and their attributes. Just keep reading for now and reserve the answer "why" for the future). I was driving in my car when my client called me to ask me if she should take the new position she was being offered in her company. Right as she's asking me the question, a yellow car cut me off. In this numerological system, there are nine numbers, and certain numbers fit certain colors; for example, there are three White numbers, which are one, eight, and siz; there is one Yellow (five); there is one Purple (nine); and so on. All yellow things can be translated or converted into number five. This yellow car appears, and it's number five. But in this art, we need two numbers to make a conclusion, so I wait a little bit, and another car appeared in front of me (two, because there are two cars); finally, I've got my two numbers, five and two. Admittedly this may seem somewhat subjective, and it can be done different ways, but it depends on your ability to see things in a different way, thanks to being in an open, receptive state.

If you're familiar with the movie *The Matrix*, there comes a point at which, when Keanu Reeves understands the idea of the Matrix and successfully changes the state of his mind, everything starts happening. We can call that "being in the alpha state," the special state of calm in your mind when internal dialogue is stopped. Being in the alpha state allows you to see the whole picture, not just parts of it. If you're in this alpha state and these two cars appear, it reveals a pattern—five and two, probably the worst combination in the Xuan Kong Chinese numerological system. Thus, my answer to her was immediately, "Don't change your job, just stay where you are."

. . . .
Student Success Story: "Feng Shui saved my son..."

Events going on around us are connected to decisions we make, even if there is no rational connection. In nature there are no conflicts. Conflicts come from false assumptions. If you merely look at the surface, sometimes there are conflicts, like "Should I follow plan A or B?" But if we take this conflict apart and analyze deeply what the purpose of it is, what it's trying to tell us, we will find the answer.

I once had a client come to me with the problem: his son had no job. In a case like this, I first try to find the root cause, why he's in that situation. It's not just as simple as "Oh, someone needs a job, we need to activate something that will bring him a job." People have the mistaken idea with Feng Shui that if someone wants some money, we simply need to activate the money star. If someone wants to have more and better sex, we need to activate sex stars. If someone wants to be healthy, they need to activate health stars. But, in fact, that's a naive way of thinking, because Feng Shui just doesn't work in that way.

We need to be more rational and more precise. Why does this guy have no job? If I start talking with him, I may discover that it's not that he's lazy but that his expectations are too high. He may have the idea that, "I'm well educated, so I should not have to take this job for which I'm too well qualified. I deserve a bigger salary and a higher position." Thus, I identify that the exact problem this client's son isn't an absence of luck but something in his character: a big ego.

Once we identify the problem, we need to change his character, and finally he will find a job. My idea in this specific case was to use Chinese metaphysics to change his character. How? One way to change somebody's character is to bring him more pain or suffering. If he has too comfortable a life, he has no impetus to change himself. So I put him in *alignment to a star we call "three green," which brings more competition and more suffering. Unpleasant events started to happen in his life, so he had a lot of disagreements with his parents, and they didn't give him money anymore. He also was separated from friends who did not support him anymore, so he had no money to buy food or beer. Finally, he decided that the situation was dire enough that he had to lower his standards, so he got a job.*

Student Success Story: A Office Change-Over

I once had a client who brought me in to consult on his house. By the time the consultation was done, it was late evening, and he insisted that I stay for a party he was having, saying that all his friends and business partners were coming, and he'd be insulted if I refused.

I decided I'd better stay. Then he said, "It will be an insult if you don't drink with me." I didn't want to insult him, so we drank quite a lot. Finally, at two in the morning his business partner asked me, "When are you leaving back to your city?" I told him, "Tomorrow morning." He said, "I've got an idea—I need you to consult on my office. Why don't we go have a look at it?" By the time we got there it was nearly three in the morning. I consulted on his office and gave him certain ideas for changing things. I positioned his desk differently and repositioned the table of his secretary, mostly just some small changes, which we did on the spot, because otherwise he would forget what I'd told him by the next day, which was Monday.

Then, the next morning, his staff showed up as usual at nine. That very day, it was discovered that his secretary, during the past two years, had sold all kinds of information to his direct competitor, so this lady was fired immediately. (It's great she was not killed. This happened in the mid-1990s in Ukraine, and it was a horrible time over here; people shot each other over stuff like that, but this guy was kind of nice.) This guy told me that this one consultation had saved him a lot of money and said, "Even if nothing but that works, it was still perfect." His life had resolved in six hours after the consultation—and we'd solved a problem he didn't even know he had.

CHAPTER TWO

Why People Fight Change

Why do human beings in general resist change, particularly when it comes to the willingness to embrace new ideas? Sometimes it's a matter of not wanting to look foolish or risk being judged as such by others. Sometimes, it's simply passivity; it's so easy to come up with the reasons for not acting, for not changing, for not opening your mind and being more accepting of new ideas.

I see that a lot in my work; people assume that Feng Shui won't work for them, because it's somehow specific to the Chinese—"It works for Chinese people but doesn't work for us"—but it's not like that. We just use Chinese characters and terminology to describe how it works. This Feng Shui terminology is convenient among Feng Shui practitioners but is not necessary at all for "Feng Shuing" your house.

In a previous chapter, I was talking about the challenge of using language to describe a phenomenon. We could make up a language that described these things. But the terminology already exists, and it exists in Chinese language, so that's what we use. It's the same as the fact that in marketing and for computers the world-over, we use English terminology, because that's where this stuff first appeared and was popularized. That's why we use Chinese terminology to describe Feng Shui. It's ancient Chinese terminology that still applies to our lives today.

Actually, the root origin of Chinese metaphysics is a science, which is called *Qi Men Dun Jia*, and which can be translated as "Mystical Doors." In ancient China, people used it during war to choose directions and times in order to protect their armies, because in certain time periods the chances of success are much better than in others. The science talks about how to escape when you're in trouble. It talks about how to prosper in negotiations and so on. Feng Shui is more or less an interpretation of Qi Men Dun Jia. It couldn't be described as modern, except in comparison with Qi Men Dun Jia because Qi Men Dun Jia appeared 25 centuries before the birth of Christ, and Feng Shui didn't appear clearly until after Christ's birth. Qi Men Dun Jia is not originally a Chinese art. It's described in Chinese characters, but it likely existed much longer, before Chinese civilization appeared. Maybe it was brought to us from another planet. Who knows?

04.07.2016   6:00

六合　　　　壬	太阴　　　　戊	腾蛇　　　　乙
8	4	6
住　　杜　　乙	冲　　景　　辛	辅　　死　　己丙
白虎　　　　庚	陰 三 癸卯	直符　　　　辛
7	辛	2
蓬　　伤　　戊	英　　景	英　　惊　　癸
玄武　　　　丁	九地　　　　癸	九天　　　　己丙
3	5	1
心　　生　　壬	柱　　休　　庚	芮禽　开　　丁

Interestingly, the perspective from which things are described might lead you to think that was actually the case, that the art came from space. In the descriptions of how planets interact with stars, for instance, the creators of Chinese metaphysics seemed to have looked at everything from the top down. There are two systems and perspectives in astronomy: one is geocentric, as things are seen from the Earth's perspective, and the other is heliocentric, as seen from the sun. These ancients used a heliocentric system, and they describe stars and planets in the way that we look at Earth from space. It's a strangely alien perspective, in which all stars and ranges of mountains and river flows are described from the top looking down. It's hard to know how they arrived at this point of view.

A lot of people are constrained by the ideas they grew up with and aren't able or willing to think in new ways. People say, "My parents did not use it, and my grandparents didn't use it. They were successful, so why should I use it?" Well, we can say that your parents didn't use iPads, and they didn't use cell phones, and they were successful, so why should we use those things? Even if our parents and grandparents didn't use ancient Feng Shui, they probably depended on some kind of folk knowledge. In Russia, in the 17th century, before they built a house, they would bring chunks of raw meat and put them on sticks everywhere in different places on the land and see where it went bad the fastest. They didn't build a house on the areas where the meat became rotten the quickest. In many countries, including the United States, dowsers search for water below the ground with forked sticks. There has always been a place in every culture for shamanistic knowledge. But our problem is that over the past hundred years or so, we have become disconnected from nature. Most of us literally don't live on the ground any more. Most of us don't farm. Some people don't even seem to have any real idea where their food comes from. They just assume it shows up on the supermarket shelves, ready to go.

THE WISDOM OF OUR ANCESTORS

We are disconnected from the nature and have forgotten much of the old wisdom of our ancestors. That's why we need to regain knowledge in order to come back to this communication with natural forces, and one of the ways to do that is to use Feng Shui. It's not an exact science, but it is more precise than many people think.

It's almost impossible to think about anything if we don't have terminology for it. You need to have precise language and terminology to understand a concept and to see from the correct perspective. It's the same for describing good and bad places to live, where to prosper, to survive, and to be happy. We need specific terminology to describe these places in detail, and Feng Shui has a profound, precise wording for everything; from that perspective alone, it's a useful art. Note that I don't call this a "science"; to me, it's more like art, because it requires more imagination and insight. (The same goes for psychology, in my opinion; I wouldn't call that a precise science. You need to have insight, empathy, and intuition to be successful as a psychologist.)

People have odd ideas of Feng Shui. Some feel that the Chinese developed it specifically as an adjunct to home design. Part of the problem is that what I call "pop Feng Shui" appeared in the 20th century, with rules delineating things for home layout, such as, "There are eight corners, or eight sectors inside of the house; the sector for wealth, sector for fame, sector for love, whatever. This wealth corner is always at the southeast direction." Now, if everybody uses the same approach and keeps their money in a southeast area of their house, that certainly makes it easy for thieves to rob your house, so you can make them wealthy—but otherwise, it's a joke. Even this concept of corners is not real Feng Shui. Feng Shui for each house is unique; you can't just generalize like that.

Another idea people have is that **Feng Shui is just a bogus new religion that's been created to siphon money from people**. I actually agree and disagree with this notion at the same time. If you look at the great Feng Shui masters of the past and study their biographies, you discover that it wasn't about money for them at all. In fact, most of them were well off to begin with. They were either ministers in Chinese government or wealthy from some other source, and they investigated and codified this law of cause and effect; why, for instance, a particular positioning of the bed creates certain results. For them, it was like an intellectual pursuit, a pastime. You've probably noticed that wealthy and successful people need to have hobbies. Sometimes it's a very expensive hobby, like golf, and they become quite enthusiastic about it, despite the fact that it costs rather than makes them money.

For these ancient masters, from the very beginning Feng Shui was a hobby, not a source of wealth. One of those was Grand Master Yang Jun Song (834AD–906AD), who died during the Tang Dynasty. Most schools of Feng Shui reference him. He's remembered for using his skills as a Feng Shui master to help the peasantry, because he visited the houses of poor farmers and did things like placing water in correct positioning to help them to survive and thrive. But from another perspective, we can agree that Feng Shui *is* just another religion that can be used to collect money from people. That said, the same could be said of Facebook and Apple and Twitter and whatever else seizes the public's fancy. They have many fans, many followers, and if something has a lot of followers it can and likely will be monetized somehow. Look at Apple; it's another form of religion. From the certain point of view, people buy Apple products not because the products are the best on the market but because they'd feel like losers if they don't buy Apple products. I'm not immune; I love Apple products. And I would never buy a Mercedes, because I'm a BMW guy.

Generally speaking, people don't like to be outside of their comfort zone. They try to keep within the walls in which they're familiar. To seek true knowledge, however, you need to change your mindset, and you need to be willing to take the risk and try new things. For some people, that is unacceptable. If your friend finds out you're talking with a Feng Shui master, he or she may think you need some medical help because you've lost your mind. Don't laugh; I've seen a lot of family issues come up because of the practice of Feng Shui.

This isn't the case in the East, of course, where Feng Shui plays into a person's decision-making processes from day one to their last day and beyond. One part of the practice still common in places such as Singapore and Taiwan is using Feng Shui for the placement of graves, to position a gravestone in the proper direction and at the proper time to bring good luck to the dead person's descendants. If, as an example, a family suffers from disease, they'll have a Feng Shui master check the graves of their parents or grandparents. If the situation of the grave is shown to be very bad—if they discover that the body is underwater, for instance—they exhume it and find another place for it and install the grave properly.

THE ART AND SCIENCE OF FENG SHUI

In Asia, there are more men than women who are interested in Feng Shui. I only know a few women who practice. They are rare, possibly partly because in ancient China it was forbidden for women to practice Feng Shui. For women, because of their monthly cycles, for three or five days in a month they are very *Yin*. When they are Yin, they are inclined to attract certain energies, so for them it was not useful, or even permitted, to practice Feng Shui.

In Western society, it's actually the opposite; more women are interested in Feng Shui science than men, and I can tell you why. If you look carefully at the history of how Feng Shui appeared in the West, from the very beginning a lot of what was discussed had to do with interior design—certain sculptures and certain pictures and colors and things of nature—which tend to be women's business. Because of this interior design orientation, more women became interested in what they saw as Feng Shui-friendly decoration and placing of Chinese-style decorations inside of their houses, hoping to channel positive energies. But this, of course, has nothing to do with real Feng Shui, and sometimes it creates disagreement because the husband wants to see his familiar, normal house without all the faux-Chinese junk scattered around. But there's no reason to be confrontational or even to share with your spouse or coworker that what you're doing is Feng Shui. You can just say you're getting bored with this table in this corner, and you would like to reposition it into another corner. There is no need to reference Feng Shui for that, to be honest; you can tell people whatever they are ready to hear. You should not tell them things that may upset them unnecessarily. That's why, generally speaking, practitioners don't talk much about the magical side of Qi Men Dun Jia, the Mystical Doors science. We talk about the scientific part. But in the actual practice, we utilize both.

Chiefly, you need to be aware of the things that are connected to each other and accept that nothing appears spontaneously in this world. One thing brings another one. That one in turn brings another one. Everything is interconnected. Some people think they're rich because they're clever or they're special. But when I examine my own success, I realize that it happens not only because of me but because of my team. Certainly it would never have happened without my teachers, nor would it ever have happened without my parents. And, of course, I'd have no chance to prosper in my business without my clients. So you can see that there are many different parts played in order to bring about a certain result.

To understand and to use Feng Shui, you need to have the mindset of interconnectedness, to understand that small changes like the shifting of your table or bed can create certain results. It's like what mathematician and meteorologist Edward Lorenz called the "butterfly effect," in which something as small as the movement of a butterfly's wings in one part of the world creates a disturbance of air that can ultimately fuel a hurricane thousands of miles away.

Most of my clients come to me looking for the kinds of adjustments that will help them make money. But that's not its only function. Feng Shui can also help couples that have problems conceiving. It has applications in helping people to get more out of their educations; some Feng Shui activations can potentially even make people smarter. If someone has no money, than he's in trouble, but it could still be worse; he could be poor and sick. But his situation could be even worse—he could be poor and sick and stupid. It can be even worse yet; someone can be poor, sick, stupid, and evil-minded then he's in real trouble. So we can use Feng Shui either to make someone a bit more healthier, a bit wealthier, whatever is needed, and improve the quality of his life.

Everyone has a reason for being resistant to admitting that something as "out there," as Feng Shui is considered for many people, might just work. Some are afraid of being laughed at by their friends. Some are afraid of being ripped off.

I try to address those clients who trust and ignore those people who don't trust. It's much easier. The fact is, a person's long-held belief system is not easy to change, and I don't need to waste my time and energy talking someone into something. In writing this book, I would rather attract those readers who can allow themselves to trust, at least a bit, and who already have some kind of interest in the topic and to push away those people who do not. They're so invested in hanging onto their rather small ideas, and so fearful of being made fools of, that they can't open their minds to any new kinds of thoughts, and those people I don't want to talk to. If you don't get this, at least to this point, you probably won't benefit, because you won't go at it with the right attitude, with the required open mind.

··

STUDENT SUCCESS STORY:
"Feng Shui is a powerful tool"

"In 2006, this is where I was in my life: an unmarried girl of 29, with a good job but no home of my own, just renting an apartment in Moscow. At this point, I'd been dabbling in Feng Shui for several years and tried to arrange everything according to it, even in the apartment I rented. For my birthday, I received a small amulet that had a picture of a nest on it (my friend told me it was a symbol of me getting my own "nest"). It wasn't Feng Shui related but a nice gesture. I just smiled, as I didn't have either plans or money for this, but I went ahead and hung it up in the eastern sector of my place. It was as though suddenly something had set the wheels in motion; I found a mortgage that didn't require any down payment and bought an apartment. It happened exactly four months after my birthday, a few days before the New Year.

I took a breath, a little amazed at this turn of fate, and started work on renovation of the apartment in accordance with the Feng Shui principles. When I finished everything, I thought that the only thing I needed to be on Cloud Nine was a family of my own—a husband and children. I had a lot of admirers, but none of them felt like Mr. Right. I tried to figure it out; what was missing in my cozy palace-studio? Or, maybe, was there something that shouldn't be there? I realized that the problem was the sofa I had bought together with my ex-boyfriend. I had kept it after our break up, which was very painful for me. Well, I needed to replace it, immediately!

In a couple of weeks, the old sofa was sold, and a new one took its place. There was no room for the past left in my apartment or my life—and in a week I met my future husband. Our son is five months old now, and I am absolutely sure that Feng Shui really is a powerful tool.

P.S. It feels a bit cramped in our home now, we need more space. I'm sure that Feng Shui will help us again and everything will be fine!"

Throughout the centuries, Chinese metaphysics in general and Feng Shui in particular were exclusive practices available only to the highest aristocracy of China, to the emperor or ministers and those close to the emperor. These arts were not available to the general public, because the emperor wished to keep them to himself. Books about the arts were prohibited. But, inevitably, information began to leak. More and more people were hearing about Feng Shui and getting interested in it. The powers that be created some simplified versions and dumbed-down information and spread them out in the general public, but they kept the more precise and strongest techniques for themselves. My Feng Shui master recently explained to me that this was our problem as Feng Shui practitioners today. We have a lot of texts, and some texts are original texts, but other texts were created relatively recently for the general public, either to fool them or to cheat them by giving them the wrong information about Feng Shui or to give them a simplified and largely useless version. Our problem is that we sometimes have no idea which is which.

Either it's a correct version or a fake version of the original text. That's why, if you don't have the direct transmission of the practices with your master, who had the teachings directly from his master, who in turn learned it directly from his master, you can't be sure that what you're getting is correct. Some knowledge is lost throughout the centuries as it is passed from one master to another master, and only through practice can they see what is working and what doesn't produce results.

That's why we cannot really successfully attain profound knowledge from books, and I'm not even talking exclusively about Feng Shui. Here's an example: Let's say there is a nuclear plant. It uses a nuclear chain reaction to create electricity. This is strictly science, and its construction can be logically, clearly described in a book. We can find a lot more information on the topic on the Internet. But let's say something happens, and all of that available information is wiped out. Now, take an engineer who's aware conceptually that such a plant could be built but has no information about how to do it and no way to consult with people who've built them in the past. To recreate that knowledge through trial and error would probably take centuries, but he can use the book and his own knowledge to complete the job. We cannot transmit all human knowledge through books. People carry knowledge; books are just support materials. Without the human element, you're lost. The same is true of Feng Shui; what can be taught through a book is limited. It's the transmission of information from master to master that is the heart of the practice.

CHAPTER THREE

The Three Kinds of Luck

There are three kinds of luck in our lives—heaven luck, earth luck, and human luck. Feng Shui can harmonize these three lucks.

Human luck concerns those things under our control. This would include the choices that we make during our life, whether to take this job or that one or to partner with this person or that one. We choose our surroundings, the neighborhoods or town in which we live. This area of free will and the choices we make is what Feng Shui is essentially talking about, just as human luck is what psychologists address.

Heaven luck is a thing that is beyond our control, elements that influence our destiny, such as who our parents are, in what country we are born, our genetic codes, and our birthdates. We can study our destiny, just as we can study astrology. We can study our strengths and weaknesses, and we can fuel our strengths and avoid fuelling our weaknesses—but we can't do much to influence heaven luck.

Earth luck is the influence of the surrounds we spend our time in, such as the house, apartment, office, café, etc.

As human beings, we exist between two forces, Heaven and Earth, and to explain our positions using Chinese philosophy, we can use Trigrams. Trigrams consist of three lines: the bottom line is connected with earth luck, the midline is connected with human luck, and the top line is connected with heaven luck.

Western society is more deeply invested in the notion of free will and choice, as described in the idea of human luck. Traditional Chinese metaphysics is concentrated more on studying heaven luck and uses earth luck to support our goals, support our dreams, or whatever. Human luck is covered in the study of Chinese astrology, whereas heaven luck is the study of date selection, choosing the most propitious days to start a business, for a grand opening, or for a marriage ceremony.

Feng Shui is about earth luck.

FENG SHUI LUCK

When Western society talks about Feng Shui, in most cases they're getting it all wrong. They're confusing earth luck with human luck, which is connected with our belief system, with forces of thinking and with the law of attraction, what that movie *The Secret* is about. This is what Tony Robbins and motivational speakers generally promote: improving ourselves by improving our belief in ourselves, which is about human luck. It's inaccurate to call these kinds of things Feng Shui.

Feng Shui has nothing to do with our belief system. It is more like the laws of physics. Let's say I have an item in my hand. If I drop it, I can predict that it will fall down. It will not fly up. And regardless of whether I believe it will fall or I believe it won't fall, it will, in fact, fall. This is a law of physics here on Earth. The same thing applies with the laws of Feng Shui. It's thought by many that in order to start practicing it or to start studying it, we need some kind of belief. But even if we totally deny the existence of those laws, the laws themselves do not cease to exist. They are independent of our belief in them, in the same way that gravity exists independent of our belief. That's why Feng Shui involves earth luck, which does not require any religion or any beliefs.

Human luck is clearly different. When you're talking about human luck, you're actually talking about preparation and attitude. It's how you face life, about the choices you make and your psychology. We tend to think of ourselves as free to choose that kind of luck. We can make whatever choice we want, can't we? But in Feng Shui, heaven luck is not like that; we can't change heaven luck at all. We can follow; we can go through doors that are open and forget about those which are closed for us in this life. We can study it and find ways to apply what we learn, but it cannot be actually changed.

There is a technique in Chinese astrology to predict someone's death using hand lines, and it's actually quite accurate. Sometimes a person's date of death can be predicted with 80 percent or 90 percent probability. But that's heaven luck, and we can't do anything to influence that, so it's not very useful knowledge at all. Our destiny is what it is; we can know it, or some of it, but we can't change it.

But we can change our Feng Shui, our earth luck, because we can change our houses and apartments and the country we live in. And we can change our behavior and manipulate these two kinds of luck (earth and human) to change the final results. Let's say I'm not born with a destiny of becoming a billionaire, so I can do nothing about that. It's heaven luck that dictates this limit. I will never have a billion dollars, but this heavenly corridor is pretty broad and can accommodate a broad range of potential outcomes, depending on you, on your actions. That's where human luck and earth luck come into play. So, let's say someone earns $2K or $3K American dollars a month but could potentially make his earnings much higher, like $30K or $100K a month. We can manipulate our destiny, using earth and human luck, and create positive results in our life **inside of this broad corridor that is predefined by our heavenly luck**.

STUDENT SUCCESS STORY: "The house in the village
brought us good luck"

"Eight years ago, I knew nothing about Feng Shui. Our family lived in a shared apartment in the center of Moscow. We had two little children, and the youngest had just been born. I didn't work and stayed with him at home, and we could hardly survive with just my husband's salary. The apartment and its inhabitants were so dreadful that I shudder with horror when I recall it. During the twelve years we had been living there, we survived two fires, one murder (in the room next door), an attack by a neighboring alcoholic with a kitchen knife during his delirium tremens episodes, and numerous

scandals and sleepless nights. In this apartment lived three more families, apart from us. We were in the waiting list for an apartment but didn't seem likely to get one.

To be able to take our children out of this hell at least for the summer, we did everything possible and managed to buy a tiny old house in a village. The house was very old, it had small windows, and its roof leaked, but at the same time it was cozy. There was a huge apple orchard around it. As soon as we moved there, our lives began to change. First, my husband was promoted at work. Next, when we came back to Moscow in autumn, I found a well-paid job in my field that allowed me to work at home so that I could stay home with my children! Three months after that, we got a new three-bedroom apartment in a very good neighborhood. I used to joke that the house in the village brought us luck. But only when I started to study Feng Shui seriously did I come to understand that it was not a joke, as the house and the place had very good Feng Shui. And it really changed our lives!"

ASTROLOGY PILLARS

Inside of the Chinese astrology chart, there are four pillars: the annual pillar, the months pillar, the day pillar, and the hour pillar. Each pillar includes two Chinese characters, one on top and one below. This one on top of each pillar—the year, month, day, and hour of our birth—is called the Heavenly Stem. The one below is called the Earthly Branch. Thus, even our astrology charts incorporate the idea that we are between Heaven and Earth. Our mind and consciousness are attached to our human luck, which as we've seen can be changed. But these two parts, Heaven and Earth, are pretty well determined by our time, date, month, and year of our birth.

There are also a few other luck pillars, like the ten-year luck pillar, in which two characters explain ten years of our life, two more characters explain ten more years, and so forth. To illustrate, we can say that my astrology chart, my four pillars, is like the car I was born with, and this ten-year luck pillar is like the road I drive on. This road can be bumpy and bad, or this road can be great. We are the drivers. We can use our chart in the wrong way or the right way. We can miss our direction. We can drink and drive. But, ideally, we can study our chart and find from it our strengths and weaknesses. Even in terms of our professional lives, we can choose which careers suit us best: administrator, businessman, nurse, or artist. We can also study our relationships on the chart, because in terms of relationships, people are not equal. Some will create great relationships. Some are only capable of failed relationships. Those who have bad relationships usually say, "Wow, there is something wrong, because my friend has a perfect life, has perfect kids, everything's perfect in his family life. But I always seem to meet the wrong woman or no woman at all, no matter how hard I try." The fact is, those relationship tendencies are visible in your chart from the very beginning, from your birth, in fact. Your chart predicts your relationships, good and bad. While it cannot be turned around 180 degrees, we can play with our chart in various ways and use it to shift our destiny in a direction that is better for us.

Let's consider a relationship: a woman is married to a man, they're more or less the same age, they have children, and they spend a lot of time together. They're happy, never divorced, have never separated, and so on. But what if this woman had married someone much older than she, who was divorced and had other kids he had to spend time and money on? Or perhaps her alternate husband might be a sailor or a long-distance truck driver, so he's gone for many months, or many weeks, so they don't find time much together, and this means this destiny of having a bad relationship is realized. Through her choice, she achieved a certain destiny. So—we can choose how we realize our destiny. Either we marry a divorced guy, a guy who is traveling all the time, or a perfect guy. Our awareness of what is predicted for us can help us think twice and make the smarter choice.

The chart can tell us that marriage is bad until a certain age, and after this age it will be okay. For people in those situations, you'd do better waiting past that age to marry. It's not a big deal to find yourself in an unhappy marriage in America or Russia, because people divorce each other freely, and you can always start over. But it was a big deal in old China, because divorce was out of the question. If I married someone back then, even if we hated each other and lived in separate rooms, we still could not separate because it was taboo in society. So it was crucial to find the right person at the right time, because you only had one chance.

HARMONIZING LUCK: GOOD QI

Feng Shui can help us to harmonize the kinds of luck in our lives. We can activate certain parts of our houses and offices to bring certain results. Take the case of a lady who's unhappy because she has no husband or boyfriend. We can activate her Peach Blossom structure by putting flowers in a certain corner on certain days to move this energy. Or we can reposition her bed to bring this Peach Blossom luck and remove this relationship block. Then, she will meet someone. Sometimes this happens pretty fast, even within a couple of weeks. Quite often, we find that a key sector in your house is blocked by furniture or by a big plant, so when we simply remove the plant or the furniture from this corner, luck improves immediately.

We can help with a money block, because we can discover which room in the house is the money room, which we can describe by a fixed Feng Shui "plate" (natal stars chart, San He), or we can describe it by a dynamic plate (annual or monthly stars etc.). This room contains a young, very active energy. You can effectively use this room for business or as a study, but you should not use it for a bedroom, because not only will its active energy keep you from sleeping well, but it will also affect your wealth. How? Because we generally keep our bedroom peaceful and quiet, so somehow we make this wealth luck sleepy and actually damage our wages. We can advise our client to use a different room for a bedroom and to use this "money room" for a home office, and we see that wealth luck improves immediately.

Instead of luck, however, we can say qi: heaven qi, earth qi, and human qi. There are three streams of qi, and good qi brings good results, while bad qi brings bad results. This feels like bad luck and good luck. Good earth luck we can call good Feng Shui. Bad earth luck, we can call bad Feng Shui.

Once, I consulted for a restaurant. They had two doors. One of them was used as the main door and the other as a sort of secondary door. The restaurant staff mostly used the second door, while the main entrance was the one customers used. Unfortunately, bad Feng Shui affected the main door. Not only was there a tree nearly in front of this door, but there was also a big garbage can nearby. Inside the building, they had a corner that also adversely affected this main door. I advised them to change the main entrance to the current staff entrance. I also chose a day on which that change should be made— and they doubled their business in the month after my consultation. It was simple advice, and I couldn't understand why they hadn't thought of it themselves before. The second door was more convenient for clients. It was better designed. But they initially resisted and asked, "Can you advise something different?" I told them, "Well, you paid me money to give you sufficient motivation to actually make a change, because just knowing that this door is better doesn't help. What really helps is actually repositioning your main entrance." The owner made a lot of money and ended up selling his business for a good profit.

A few years ago, a client of my colleague asked me if Feng Shui could help to get a Russian visa for her boyfriend, because her boyfriend was from Georgia, and he couldn't get a visa to Russia. He was going to have to return the next day to Georgia, so they'd have been separated and their great love destroyed. I told her, "Well, we'll try."

In those years in Feng Shui, we were talking about certain qi patterns and called them "flying stars"—just to name certain bodies of qi. Flying star attributes are nine numbers: one through nine. These numbers represent certain stars and certain qi patterns. There are five elements in Chinese metaphysics: Earth, Metal, Water, Wood, and Fire. That year, star number 9 was a north, and this star number 9 represents fire elements. This 9 star is related to foreigners and foreign countries, expansion and new beginnings, and new opportunities.

I advised her to put a candle on the north, and I used my knowledge to calculate her an hour at which she needed to light it. Within one hour after this activation, the embassy called her boyfriend and told him that he'd actually been granted the visa. I'm not suggesting that's a typical result—it does not always happen like that—but that was certainly a great success story for Feng Shui and my practice.

ALIGNING OUR LUCK

One way to think about Feng Shui's effect on your life is to imagine your car's wheel alignment. If the wheels are not properly aligned, one wheel goes one direction, and another wheel goes another direction. Your tires get destroyed pretty fast, and even your engine can get trashed. We can say the same about our lives. Let's say that our earth luck is going in one direction and that our human luck is going in a different direction. When there's no alignment in our lives, nothing works properly, and we're left sick, unhappy, and poor. We need to balance these things first in order to achieve the best outcome via our heaven luck or destiny, to pick our goals, and then to arrange our surroundings to support them.

Our furniture and our house have to be properly arranged to support our objectives, whatever they are. We need to have the information that will allow us to pick the most propitious dates for new projects, regardless of whether they are business projects or personal projects. Then we need to put our energy—our human luck and our belief system—to work on this goal, to study psychology, and to learn about our inner being. This creates the perfect alignment, allowing us to reach our goals more quickly. Nothing stops us.

Otherwise, we're apt to go down the wrong road and get stuck there. Let's say you become an adherent of the Tony Robbins motivational programs because you're trying to start a new business—but your destiny is not about being a businessman. Unfortunately, that means that you will likely never succeed in your business endeavor. Or you might choose to work for a big company and expect that you'll use the corporate ladder to get to the top in a few years. But if your Feng Shui is working against you—if your home or apartment is improperly arranged to support your business or career—you will fail, regardless of how many Tony Robbins seminars you attend. (I'm just using Tony as a common reference for the motivational speaking and personal-development industry. Please understand me correctly. I'm not attacking Tony in any way. He is a really great guy. I'm just saying that any type of psychology has obvious limitations that people are blind to.) The problem is that Tony's only talking about human luck, but we also need to bring those two other forces—the heaven luck and earth luck—and put them all together working in the same direction in order to make our goals reachable.

CHAPTER FOUR

Feng Shui and the Home

The best time to assess the Feng Shui of a house or an apartment is before you buy or rent it. It's much easier to choose a favorable home or an office space than it is to fix a bad one, because not everything about a "bad" house can be fixed. It's like your health; it's better to prevent an illness and keep yourself healthy than to try and cure an illness. I make my living as a consultant working with people whose homes, apartments, or offices are not properly aligned, and I do my best to help them cure these "sick" spaces. Essentially, consultants all work with places people already have, and we treat them somehow, but **they would all have much better results if they had invited us for a consultation before they moved in or, better yet, before they bought those houses.**

The first thing to consider is the area in which the home or office is located. Neighborhoods have negative influences or positive influences, and selecting a "healthy" neighborhood can save you a lot of time and effort down the line.

Apartments are often based on an L-shape floor plan. In such an arrangement, it's easy to see where the corners will meet and, depending on what each corner means, we can project the future of the family when they move in. Let's say the northwest corner is missing, located in the kitchen area with the oven in the northwest, or it meets in a bathroom. Typically, this means that the father of this family, or the family head, is weak, missing, or will be absent from this house. Perhaps he'll have to travel a lot, but the main point is that he won't be there. If you pick a house like that, it means that from the very beginning, your husband will either be missing most of the time or weak. This influence won't be seen immediately, but over a period of three or four years, its effects will be powerfully felt. Let's say a couple moves in; for two or three years things will be relatively okay—but after three years they will begin to have quarrels, and within four years divorce will probably follow. Within that initial period of about three years, something could potentially be done to bring those relationships back on track, but by the time four years have passed, something will have happened, and the family breakup will be inevitable.

If you look at a typical multistory building, normally the kitchen is located in the same room on each story, and the floor plan is the same on every floor. Your kitchen range will be exactly where your upstairs and downstairs neighbors' ranges are, as most people don't move them when they move in. But where your oven is placed is more important than you might think.

Let's talk a little about the influence of your kitchen range. Let's say it's located in a bad combination of flying stars (e.g. combo 9-5, as known from the study of Feng Shui), which brings health issues, such as blood diseases and high blood pressure or heart disease. In this position, it can also influence people to become substance abusers, alcoholics, or drug addicts. If a family lives in this apartment over a period of ten years or so, you can track what has happened to them over that time. If it's a five-story building, you can track the history of the five families in apartments located one above each other. In this case, you're likely to discover that in one of those apartments, a child has leukemia. In another family, a man has high blood pressure and heart disease and is an alcoholic. In another family, there is something else related directly back to these issues; thus, we see that people in all five families have diseases connected with this bad range position and 9-5, which is calculated using the year of construction of the building and its facing direction.

The scenario I've outlined above may sound far-fetched to you, but it's actually a story from one of my consultations. When I investigated it, I discovered that one family who lived in the same room plan didn't have any problems, which I found surprising. It turned out that just after they moved into this apartment, they did a renovation, and they repositioned their oven, so that it wasn't in a line with those in the rest of the building. In doing so, they inadvertently used a different qi pattern and created a different star combination. They didn't ask for any Feng Shui consultation before doing it, but they got lucky, and so they have none of those 9-5 issues (bad health, etc.).

There are Yin and Yang places in our homes and apartments. Yin places represent health and relationship; for instance, the bedroom is a Yin place, which symbolizes our relationships and health. Our home office rooms or our apartment door locations are Yang places, which represent career and cash flow.

STUDENT SUCCESS STORY: "There is no BS between Yin and Yang; Yin and Yang are in harmony!"

"This happened four years ago. It was our company's birthday, and two interns came to my office, with congratulations and a gift—a clock. On the dial there was a Yin and Yang picture and words: 'Yin', 'Yang', and between them bullshit' was written. I laughed and thanked the guys, and set the clock in a prominent spot in my office. Everyone who came in smiled when they saw it. 'Well! Whose idea was this?' visitors asked.

Shortly after, I had to announce an urgent planning meeting: deals had begun to fall through, and clients were suddenly all dissatisfied. I got tough with my employees and told them that the next day I'd be waiting for their suggestions on how to turn things around. One of my managers came to my office right after that meeting. She hesitated and then said, 'Have you heard of Feng Shui? Because I think we should try it.'

'Yes, I have, but I'm not going to get into the occult.'

'This is not the occult—this is Chinese metaphysics. I know a lot of successful companies that use it, and I've experienced its effects personally, twice. And I think we can change the situation with our company for the better if we use it. Please think about it! And ... can I take this clock away? There is no BS between Yin and Yang; Yin and Yang are in harmony.'

I shrugged. 'I don't know about Feng Shui, but there's always some kind of BS between a man and a woman. If this is all you wanted to say, you can go now.' When I was at home I thought about this conversation. What was so wrong with that clock that I had to get rid of it? I started to recall all the bad things that had begun to happen, right after I got the gift.

That same evening, when we celebrated our company's birthday, two light bulbs exploded, one in my office and one in our accountant's office. Within two days afterward, the negotiations I'd planned for so long fell through. My employees had to redo the same sign two times. We had no orders for a week. I began to have problems with my blood pressure, which I'd never had before and so on and on and on.

I opened the newspaper to check our ad, and right next to it was an ad for Feng Shui consultation. All night long, my manager's words flashed through my mind, especially one of them: harmony.

When I came to the office in the morning I found a resignation letter from my best specialist. That was the last straw. I went to the manager:

'Okay, let's try it, Lena.' She agreed to call a friend who was studying Feng Shui.

When her friend came to my office, she asked to take away the clock, and then we rearranged all the furniture in my office and my employees' desks, too. From that day on, the situation went back to normal and subsequently even improved further. The business was successful again. This was the first time I experienced this miracle. Later, I met a Ba Zi professional. She suggested changing where I lived, which I hadn't even considered and warned me about my future divorce, about changes in my sphere of activity, etc. Now I live in accordance with Feng Shu principles and study Feng Shui."

BED POSITIONING

There are some simple rules for things like bed positioning that anyone can follow. The first one is that we should avoid sleeping with our legs pointing in the direction of the bedroom door. Chinese people call that a *corpse position*. If there's something wrong with your bed's position, you are likely to suffer either from health or relationship issues. Those issues may lead you to depression and ultimately poor work performance, of course, which will also impact your cash flow, but you'll find it started from a problem with either relationships or health. I have a friend who's been sleeping in "corpse position" for twenty years; he's still alive, but his private life and relationships are very turbulent.

In some Feng Shui books in which the authors discuss bad and good bed directions, they talk about Gua numbers and how to calculate your Gua number. This theory is based on your birth year and uses a simple formula or tables to calculate which Gua number you belong to. Guas like 1-3-4-9 belong to the east group. Guas like 2-6-7-8 belong to the west group. For those whose Gua numbers fall into the east group, good bed directions are northeast, southeast, and south. For those in the west group, good directions are southwest, west, northwest, and northeast. For me, this theory is simplistic and ineffective.

But what does work, again, is alignment of different factors and their cumulative effect. There are eight directions. Four of them are good, and four of them are bad. Each one gets certain meanings: one of those is called Life Threatening, one of them is called 5 Ghosts, one of those is called 6 Demons, etc. If your bed direction is 5 Ghosts, and your bedroom direction is 5 Ghosts, and your apartment door is 5 Ghosts, the effect multiplies, and finally that will bring a negative consequence in your life: bankruptcy, or severe diseases, or relationship issues.

The rules used to correctly calculate your good or bad direction are more complex. In Feng Shui, we talk about forms and formulas. Formulas are related to the bedroom and to directional factors, and we need to use a compass to calculate formulas. Forms, on the contrary, describe what's around us and just seen by eyes, so we don't need to use any compass. Generally speaking, we avoid mirrors in the bedroom, because those mirrors disturb the Yin and Yang of the bedroom. Normally, in relationships, people who have a lot of mirrors in the bedroom are not stable; love triangles are apt to occur, for instance.

In general, you should avoid sleeping just under the beam, because it's like a pressure on us from above. We should also usually avoid positioning our bed to the wall of our bathroom. Having a toilet 20 or 30 centimeters away from your head on the other side of the wall is not ideal. The same goes for having a large waste pipe in the wall near your head.

It's crucial to consider these things and properly assess the home *before* you move. It's not the first thing on most people's minds when they're house hunting, but it should be. It's okay if it's an apartment, where they can move in for a short period of time and then move to another place. But if it's a family house and a place you hope to live for a longer period of time, it's better not to choose places like that to begin with.

Another issue with homes is what we call star 5 Yellow. As I have said earlier, there are nine stars with numbers 1–9, and one of these is quite dangerous. Star 5 Yellow is technically what's called the Emperor Star. It's the strongest one, and it brings huge prosperity, but it's also quite dangerous to be wrong in the presence of the emperor. If you say or do something the emperor doesn't like, you're likely to die. Most people aren't that accomplished at diplomacy and have no clue how to play with this 5 Yellow, which is where they put themselves into peril. If you really know what you're doing, you'll be quite successful, but if you don't know, there is danger. That's why, for beginners or intermediate students, in fact even the highest level of students, we normally tell them "Don't use the 5 Yellow."

2014

SE	S		SW
3	8	1	
2	4	6	
7	9	5	

E ... W

NE ... N ... NW

2015

SE	S	SW
2	7	9
1	3	5
6	8	4

E · W

NE · N · NW

2016

SE	S	SW
1	6	8
9	2	4
5	7	3

E · W

NE · N · NW

2017

9	5	7
8	1	3
4	6	2

SE · S · SW

E · W

NE · N · NW

Let's say you're going to rent an apartment or a house, and you have annual 5 Yellow on your main door, or there is a 5 Yellow on the sitting of your house (the sitting or back side is that which is opposite to the front-facing part of the house). Let's say your house faces east, and the opposite of east is west. Five is west in 2015, so don't move into a house that faces a west-east axis.

If you already own your house, you'll have to work around it. It's likely that it has two or three other doors, so don't use the west door in 2015; use a different one.

The problem is, especially in a competitive real estate market, it's nearly always easier to rent out or sell a house that has 5 Yellow in the back side or one which has 5 Yellow on the main door. Why?—because there are many more people with bad luck than people with good luck. So, if your house has bad luck, it can actually attract more buyers. You know, unconsciously they smell the bad luck somehow, like flies smell something nasty and cluster on it. It's a kind of a nasty door, and it attracts big crowds of bad luck.

But, for yourself, stay away from such a house unless you're a high-level Feng Shui master. Even if that's the case, it's still quite dangerous to play with. You could wind up with cancer or go bankrupt. Even if you're starting out with a great income and at the top level of your profession, you'll find that you must go through a very difficult time in your life, and everything will be destroyed, and you'll have a very tough lesson to learn. You may prosper afterward, if you have learned the lesson. Let's say you lost a couple of million dollars; you could potentially earn $20 million in a few years, but those few years can be very difficult. That's why we don't advise people to take that kind of risk. That said, if you have nothing to lose, if your life is already stagnant, you could opt to use this 5 Yellow; you can even activate this 5 Yellow if you're in the mood to risk self-destruction. It's a lottery. But if you get lucky and it works, your life will be great. As I said, though, we don't normally advise it. If we did, our consultant practice would be in bad shape because after such a consultation, if something bad happened immediately, those clients would blame us even if we had warned them from the beginning that they'd have to go through a very dark period of their lives in order to come out into the light on the other side. Only after a certain level of suffering can you find your way to success. People don't normally like that. They like to improve their lives or to increase their income 10 percent or 20 percent, and they're happy; they don't like to go through suffering for a couple years, even if it means they ultimately quadruple their income.

Sometimes, apartment houses actually present chains of 5 Yellow, in which the front door, the door to your apartment, and your bedroom door, for instance, are lined up. Depending on their orientation and the year, this can mean your bad luck is multiplied. I had a client in a year in which 5 Yellow was in the southeast sector. Her bedroom door faced southeast, the apartment's entry door was southeast, and the main entrance was facing southeast also, which created three times 5 Yellow.

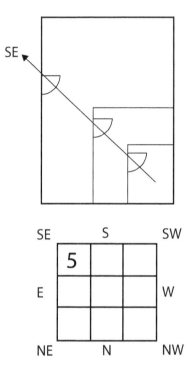

This client lost her business, she had some serious health issues, and her career was almost destroyed. That drove her to consult with me. I looked at her situation and explained what had happened; that year she moved to another apartment, and slowly everything became better.

A great deal of our luck and the luck we find in our homes can be explained by sectors, not only with missing southwest but with all stars, not only 5 Yellow. Let's say there is a sector Kun missing. Sector Kun is a technical term for the southwest sector, and that southwest sector is concerned with women, in this case the woman in the home. If the sector Kun is missing, a woman living in this place will find that she has no affinity with this house and feels uncomfortable there, so she'd rather spend her time in the office or in the nearest café. That's why we find that families living in homes with that missing southwest sector Kun often have a lot of issues. I knew a man who was married to a woman for about three years, after which she left him and went off with his business partner. Then he found a second wife, who moved in with him into the same apartment, but in one year they also separated. The problem was the apartment and its missing sector Kun. No woman could feel comfortable or happy there for long.

The star we refer to as 8 White is called the Official Money Star. It's not like big money where you're making a fortune in business, but it's more like a steady salary to support your lifestyle. It's great for employees but not so much for the business owner. This 8 White in 2015 is located in the north. If you're planning to rent your apartment for just a short period of time, and you don't care about energies for longer than one year, this is a great star. Let's say from your bedroom looking out is in the north sector in 2015, and that if you do compass measurements from your bedroom looking out, you find your front door is located in the north sector as well. There's a huge bonus if your elevator or a crossroad outside of your house is also in the north sector. Then you have a triple 8, with money, money, money. During this year, you'll have a great income, not up there with Bill Gates, of course, but a more than sufficient income with which to support your family.

INSTRUCTIONS

Measurement for this technique you have to make by a compass from the center of the apartment / private house.

1. Stand with the compass in the center of the apartment / private house. In case of flats / private homes of irregular shape, for example, T-shaped, you draw additional perimeter to the correct shape. The point of intersection of the diagonals will be the center.

2. Standing in the center, choose a visible point on the outer perimeter of the apartment / private home and measure the degree of its direction (azimuth measurement principle)

3. Note that point on the plan of the apartment / private house, sign the degree of it in its direction and navigate to it perpendicular from the center.

4. impose a template of 24 mountains on the plan of the apartment * / private house.

Template Center 24 mountains must be aligned with the center of the apartment / private house.

Find on the template 24 mountains degree measurement of the compass.

Turn template 24 until the moment when measured by compass degree on the template does not coincide with the point marked on the plan. 24 Mountain template and their degrees you will find on page 80.

5. Find the right sector. See the example on page 2.

* 24 Mountain - is a term that is used in Feng Shui to indicate 15-degree sector of the compass. Each of the eight points of light (north, south, southeast, etc.), which corresponds to 45 degrees, divided into three equal subclusters by 15 degrees. These sub-clusters are called north-1, North 2, north-3, South-1, South-2, South-3, etc.

As I've said, with this technique we do our initial measurements from our bedroom door as our starting reference point. But what if you have a place with multiple bedrooms? That means that everyone who lives in the house will have a different annual "clock." If we do measurements from your room, your door can be northeast, but if we measure from your son's room, it can be northwest. Life luck is great for you in a particular year, but it's crappy for him in that same year.

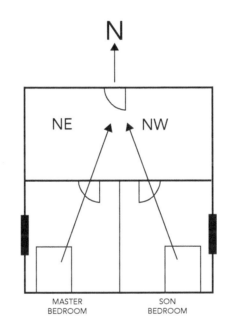

There can also be, as I've learned, a domino effect, like a chain reaction. What I've found with Feng Shui is that to produce a great result, you should have a chain. Everything should be in alignment. Let me give you an example. Le's say that you take the compass measurement on your bedroom door and find that it's located on the north; your bedroom door brings you wealth and luck in 2015. But if we measure the door to your apartment, and it's not north—say, for instance, it's west—that brings bad luck for 2015. You measure the door to your elevator and find that it's southwest (we are talking about 2015) too—one which brings good luck; not money luck but intelligent luck and study luck; you're at your brightest. Then you look outside and see a northwest crossroad, and that brings peach blossom luck, new relationships, and love.

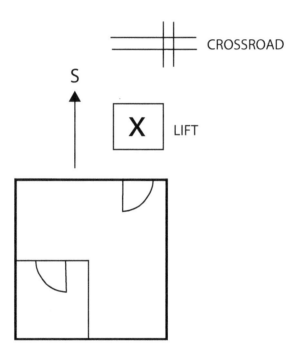

So you have the big picture: your luck is mixed, it's Black and White and Green and Yellow. Some periods during this year are great for money, but then we have a disease, and then we have a Peach Blossom love story from which we contract a sexually transmitted disease; we have great achievements in our studies, we make some more money, and then we have a car accident. You see what I'm trying to say? Because there is no alignment, there is no consistency, and you're stuck on a roller coaster of luck that's all highs and lows. The best strategy in Feng Shui is to find this alignment, to find this consistency, and to put our energy or our goals in one line, so that then we have a strong confluence of luck and a far more predictable positive result.

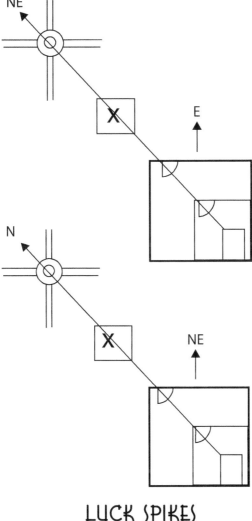

LUCK SPIKES

To have very good luck, we need to have some huge spikes in our luck; some peaks. Thus, we need to make your luck "spike," to bring it way up for a period of time, because it will stay there for longer than that period.

If you find that confusing, think about the Space Shuttle; to launch it and to get it into its orbiting position takes a great deal of fuel. But after it's in orbit, its fuel needs are really minimal. It's set in its direction and needs only small corrections, if any, to keep it in its orbit. It's the same with Feng Shui: we need to have a very great amount of energy in a short period of time to find a new orbit in our lives, and then we can relax for a certain period of time, so it's not like we always need to deal with Feng Shui. For me, Feng Shui is like a vehicle that takes you where you need to go; let's say this year I strongly desire to get from point A to B, so I use Feng Shui, like I'd use a rental car, to bring me from A to point B. After that, I can give the car back to the rental company and forget about it until I need to make another trip. I just stay in this point B and enjoy my life for a time, until I find I need to get to point C. Then I can rent another car with a full tank of gas for this second trip, and again, turn it in. There's no need for me to keep the car in the interim.

You can't plot every second of your life according to Feng Shui; there are so many other things going on that even I, who makes a living from it, don't spend all my waking hours thinking about it. If you study a martial art, you may practice it a couple of times a week, but you don't use it unless you find yourself in a position where you actually need to fight. The same goes for Feng Shui. It's a tool. We break it out and use this tool when we need it, but except for when we need it, we just forget it. I use it much more for my friends and clients than I do for myself; I'm not going to shift my bed and table around every day, after all. You just find a better position for a longer period of time and move it there, then forget about it.

Some of my clients have more than one house or multiple offices with a lot of local branches. I have to go to each of their homes or their office locations and check out each place, which is a lot of work.

If they have only one house, they probably only need one or two assessments each year: a bigger initial Feng Shui assessment but a less intensive one once or twice every year after that, because their goals or situation may have changed, or there may have been construction on their street that changes the energy in that sector. That's all that kind of client needs, although we do impart a lot of knowledge through those assessments. The big business clients have many more things to consider, like finding the best dates and times at which to schedule important deals, negotiations, or grand openings. Date selection knowledge, unlike Feng Shui, is a tool we need to use much more frequently, but that's another topic and beyond the scope of this book.

If you get too wrapped up in Feng Shui, it can turn into something like paranoia and leave you freaking out about every little decision; is now a good time to go to the bathroom? Is it a good day to get a haircut? **There are two opposing and equally foolish wrong approaches. One approach is not giving any attention at all to Feng Shui, which is very wrong and dangerous. The opposite one is to give too much attention to it, and those people probably need some medical help more than they need another consultation.**

I've seen some bad things happen to people who were affected by the negative version of the domino effect. I had one client who moved with her son into a new apartment she'd bought, in February 2005. Their front door was located northwest and was the only entrance. Her bedroom door was also in a northwest location, and there was a bad star 5 Yellow location that year. The nine stars go in cycles, and every nine years they come back to the same position. In 2005, we had the same stars as we have in 2014. The direction of her apartment door was literally life threatening. There are certain dangerous directions, based on your birth year and based on your chart, and they have certain meanings. Also, there was a bad star in her bedroom. I had several consultations during the day when I went to assess her apartment, and my assistant made notes on each of them. Over the next couple of weeks, I recorded those notes, dictating them into a recorder along with my advice on how to work with what I saw. My assistant would then transcribe those recordings for the clients. That meant that there was a two-week gap between me starting my assessment and compass measurements of her apartment and me giving her my advice. In this case, that gap proved to be fatal; she and her boyfriend had a car accident in which she was killed, although her boyfriend was not injured. This example, grim as it is, illustrates the power of multiple negative alignments. If we're talking about just one bad thing, it's okay; we'll survive. **But a chain of negative alignments can create a fatal domino effect and lead to tragic results like this.**

We should not be afraid of Feng Shui, because one or two bad things won't be likely to cause you that level of harm; probably you will simply be in a bad mood or have a cough, or your kid will do poorly in class. **When it gets dangerous is when so many things line up against you.** That's why it's important to be aware; it's likely that other things, like that client's moving date to that apartment, were also working against her. Her astrology chart might have warned her that that day was an unlucky one for her. Had she had only one or two negatives working against her, her car accident would probably just have been a fender bender, rather than a fatal one.

We share stories like this because they speak to our fears; just look at the news on television, which is almost never about someone's good luck or success. Another explanation is because it can be much easier to identify bad things and analyze them after they've happened. It's much easier to find satisfactory explanations, because people don't think as much about their good luck as they do about their bad fortune. A relatively peaceful year brings a shrug when you recollect it—but one in which several awful things happened is one you'll tell your friends about. We're not as appreciative as we probably should be; sometimes, boring is great!

CHAPTER FIVE
....

Stars That Bring Life Changes

What effect do the stars have on our lives? In the language of Feng Shui and in Chinese astrology, they're an energy presence. Depending on whether we're talking about them in astrological or Feng Shui terms, each star can have a very different meaning and require a different terminology. If we are talking about stars in Feng Shui, these are either what are called the flying stars (which are represented by numbers one through nine), or the wandering stars, which are the eight stars used in the Eight Mansions School of Feng Shui.

Some confusion can arise because, in Chinese metaphysics, we use the same word for different things, and we use different words for the same thing, so it's vitally important from the beginning to clarify what we mean and which terminology we're using. The explanation for how this system works is quite complex and rather beyond the scope of this book, but in very simple terms, Feng Shui uses a template called the 24 Mountain Chart to map our house. Each direction is divided by three, so actually there are eight main directions (south, north, east, west, northeast, northwest, southeast, and southwest), multiplied by three, which creates 24 sub-directions or the so-called 24 Mountains of Feng Shui. And because each direction is 45 degrees divided by three, it creates 15 degrees for each subsector. They often are called, South 1, South 2, South 3, or Southwest 1, Southwest 2, Southwest 3, etc.

But in original Chinese metaphysics, we use the Chinese characters to represent each of those 24 directions, represented as twelve animals; Rat, Ox, Tiger, Dragon, Rabbit, Snake, Horse, Goat, Monkey, Rooster, Dog, and Pig, along with eight Heavenly Stems and four Trigrams.

24 Mountain Chart and its correlation with a compass.

"24 mountains" is a term and a tool used in Feng Shui to define 15-degree sectors of a compass. Each direction (North, South, South East, etc.) corresponds to a 45-degree sector and is divided into three equal parts of 15 degrees. These subdirections are called North-1 (N1), North-2 (N2), North-3 (N3), South-1 (S1), etc.

DIRECTION	24 MOUNTAINS				DEGREES
SOUTH	S1	BING	丙	YANG FIRE	157.6 - 172.5
	S2	WU	午	HORSE (YANG FIRE)	172.6 - 187.5
	S3	DING	丁	YIN FIRE	187.6 - 202.5
SOUTHWEST	SW1	WEI	未	GOAT (YIN FIRE)	202.6 - 217.5
	SW2	KUN	坤	SOUTHWEST (EARTH)	217.6 - 232.5
	SW3	SHEN	申	MONKEY (YANG METAL)	232.6 - 247.5
WEST	W1	GENG	庚	YANG METAL	247.6 - 262.5
	W2	YOU	酉	ROOSTER (YIN METAL)	262.6 - 277.5
	W3	XIN	辛	YIN METAL	277.6 - 292.5
NORTHWEST	NW1	XU	戌	DOG (YANG EARTH)	292.6 - 307.5
	NW2	QIAN	乾	NORTHWEST (METAL)	307.6 - 322.5
	NW3	HAI	亥	PIG (YIN WATER)	322.6 - 337.5
NORTH	N1	REN	壬	YANG WATER	337.6 - 352.5
	N2	ZI	子	RAT (YANG WATER)	352.6 - 7.5
	N3	GUI	癸	YIN WATER	7.6 - 22.5
NORTHEAST	NE1	CHOU	丑	OX (YIN EARTH)	22.6 - 37.5
	NE2	GEN	艮	NORTHEAST (EARTH)	37.6 - 52.5
	NE3	YIN	寅	TIGER (YANG WOOD)	52.6 - 67.5
EAST	E1	JIA	甲	YANG WOOD	67.6 - 82.5
	E2	MAO	卯	RABBIT (YIN WOOD)	82.6 - 97.5
	E3	YI	乙	YIN WOOD	97.6 - 112.5
SOUTHEAST	SE1	CHEN	辰	DRAGON (YANG EARTH)	112.6 - 127.5
	SE2	XUN	巽	SOUTHEAST (WOOD)	127.6 - 142.5
	SE3	SI	巳	SNAKE (YIN FIRE)	142.6 - 157.5

Basically, these stars of energy patterns bring us certain opportunities. Let's say we are talking about the Nobleman star. We look into our Chinese astrology chart and follow our own Nobleman stars, the animals of which are the Goat and Ox.

Day Master			Noble Man Star	
甲 Jia Yang Wood	戊 Wu Yang Earth	庚 Geng Yang Metal	丑 Chou Ox	未 Wei Goat
乙 Yi Yin Wood		己 Ji Yin Earth	子 Zi Rat	申 Shen Monkey
丙 Bing Yang Fire		丁 Ding Yin Fire	亥 Hai Pig	酉 You Rooster
壬 Ren Yang Water		癸 Gui Yin Water	卯 Mao Rabbit	巳 Si Snake
辛 Xin Yin Metal			午 Wu Horse	寅 Yin Tiger

Nobleman Star

Day Master	Noble Man Star
甲 Yang Wood	Ox and Goat
戊 Yang Earth	
庚 Yang Metal	Rat and Monkey
乙 Yin Wood	
己 Yin Earth	
丙 Yang Fire	Pig and Rooster
丁 Yin Fire	
壬 Yang Water	Rabbit and Snake
癸 Yin Water	
辛 Yin Metal	Horse and Tiger

The Goat represents Southwest 1, and the Ox is a Northeast 1, and if it activates, whether that happens by renovation or by water, it brings us into contact with noble people, perhaps powerful teachers and mentors. It could be that we need a good doctor who can recognize what's troubling our health or perhaps a Bill Gates or Warren Buffet who gives us great business advice. That's why they call this the Nobleman star.

We can use the Feng Shui part either with or without date selection. When it's used without date selection, it will still bring results—but if those patterns are activated on a bad day, then the result can be mixed. Let's say our Nobleman sector is activated—but it's on a less than optimal day, by which I mean the energy of the date itself is broken. In that case, this Nobleman sector being activated brings us noble people who give us great advice, but it is a "sideways and back." In other words, things that aren't so great will happen in conjunction with the appearance of the noblemen. Perhaps they or we will become ill at around the same time that you meet them. That's why it's a wise idea to combine the Feng Shui part with the date selection part, so we avoid most of the sideways effects. Probably not all of them can be avoided, however, because in a sense there is a tradeoff; if you want to get something, you have to pay something. The trick is to do what you can to make sure that the sideways effects are relatively minor and affordable for us. For instance, we might have the flu as a sideways effect but not a heart attack. That's the difference.

In order to find our own stars, like Peach Blossom, Traveling Horse, or Nobleman, we can use either the year of our birth or date of our birth. If we use the date of our birth, we need to have a special calculator or a special table. If you visit my website at www.ba-zi. com, you'll find a calculator that allows you to put in your date, hour, and month of your birth. It will tell you what the sectors are for these powerful forces: which sector is Nobleman, which sector is Peach Blossom, and which is Traveling Horse for you.

THE TRAVELING HORSE

The Traveling Horse is one of the Ba Zi symbolic stars. Few people know, however, that it is possible to use it to select auspicious dates in Feng Shui, too. Every person has two Traveling Horse stars: one for the year of birth, and one for the day of birth.

Chart 1 of the Traveling Horse looks like this:

Year/Day Branch			Traveling Horse
Shen Monkey	Zi Rat	Chen Dragon	Yin (Tiger)
Hai Pig	Mao Rabbit	Wei Goat	Si (Snake)
Yin Tiger	Wu Horse	Xu Dog	Shen (Monkey)
Si Snake	You Rooster	Chou Ox	Hai (Pig)

THE TRAVELING HORSE
AND THE DAY OF YOUR BIRTH

Being a symbolic star, the Traveling Horse in Ba Zi symbolizes quick decisions and actions, change of the place of residence, and traveling. If you study the chart above, you will see the principle of defining this star. The Traveling Horse star will always be an animal that encounters and pushes the first animal of the triangle.

Year/Day Branch		
Shen	Zi	Chen
Monkey	Rat	Dragon
Hai	Mao	Wei
Pig	Rabbit	Goat
Yin	Wu	Xu
Tiger	Horse	Dog
Si	You	Chou
Snake	Rooster	Ox

This is the essence of the Traveling Horse—to push, to mobilize, to spur into action every process, every stagnant case.

In Ba Zi forecasting, we look at the location of the Traveling Horse star. For instance, if the Traveling Horse star is located in the day branch, we can say that a person will probably meet his or her future spouse in a journey. If a Traveling Horse star is in the Earth Branch of an hour, it is responsible for actions, psychology, and emotions. The person can be very active and makes decisions quickly, perhaps acting first and thinking afterward. This person probably moves or travels a lot, is likely to change jobs frequently or get a career promotion, or will change the city or country in which they live.

When it is in the Traveling Horse ten-year Luck Pillar (register for free and put your date of birth into the Ba Zi calculator ba-zi. com), you should be ready for a journey, for a change of your place of residence or even a new city or country. We study the reasons why this is so in the context of the Ba Zi pillar this star comes into contact with.

Here's a table of the symbolic stars for
the Ba Zi chart just below it:

Symbolic stars	Day branch	Year branch
Peach Blossom	子 Zi Rat	卯 Mao Rabbit
Traveling Horse Star	巳 Si Snake	申 Shen Monkey
Academic Star	壬 Wu Horse	亥 Hai Pig
Nobleman Star	子 ZI Rat 申 Shen Monkey	丑 Chou Ox 未 Wei Goat

THE TRAVELING HORSE STAR FOR SELECTING DATES

When we select auspicious dates, the Traveling Horse star helps to speed up the event for which we choose the date and time.

For example, if we need to get matters off the ground quickly, we should select an hour of the Traveling Horse in relation to the Day Branch. Keep in mind the need to avoid a clash between the Earthly branch of the day and the Earth Branch of the hour.

If you see such a clash, you should pick another hour. This is the general rule of date selection. If a Day Branch was not 申 Shen, but 辰 Chen or 子 Zi, the 寅 Yin hour would also be the hour of the Traveling Horse for this day and with no clash.

THE TRAVELING HORSE STAR IN FENG SHUI

The most interesting part of implementing the knowledge about this symbolic star is using the Traveling Horse star in Feng Shui.

We have this star in our homes. Actually, there are two of them. One is the Traveling Horse star, and it is calculated in relation to the Year Branch of a person. This one is used in Feng Shui. What do we use it for? To spur into action a stagnant case or a delayed process, to accelerate sale of a piece of real estate, to change the place of residence, to finally start a long-awaited journey that was for some reason delayed, or to depart to take up permanent residence in another country.

For this, you'll need to find a sector of the Traveling Horse in your house or apartment.

FINDING A SECTOR OF THE TRAVELING HORSE

For instance, in the example above there is 巳 Si, Snake in the Earth Branch of the year. For 巳 Si (Snake), the Traveling Horse star is 亥 Hai (Pig). Let's find the Pig sector on the map of your apartment. To do this, we need to stand in the center of the apartment with a compass and see where in the outer perimeter there is a 15 degrees sector of the Hai, northwest 3. We will use this sector for an activation with a fountain or a burning candle at a proper (selected) day and hour.

But in the space, there is one more Traveling Horse that is calculated directly for a house or an apartment. The space is like a living organism that also has its stars, both symbolic and flying. And when we refer to ambitious targets like changes in life and in the place of residence, it's good to use this sector.

In order to find the Traveling Horse sector for your house or apartment, use a metaphysical approach. Take a compass, stand in the center of a house/apartment and measure the direction of the entrance door. Then see Chart 1 to find the Traveling Horse, in relation to the Earthly branch, for the sector* a compass showed.

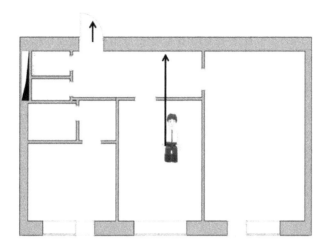

*Look for the correlation of an ordinary compass measurements with the Earthly branches *in Chapter 5.*

Let's say that measurements we made in the center of the house/ apartment show that the middle of the entrance door is 220 degrees, the Kun mountain. The Kun trigram has neither symbolic stars nor Heavenly Stems (甲,乙,丙, etc.), so we should look at San He double mountains. Or, even easier, we can look at the next Earth Branch at the compass (or 24 mountain compass). The next after Kun is 申 Shen. For Shen, the Traveling Horse star is 寅Yin, northwest 3.

An important note: These sectors should not contain any cumbersome furniture like wardrobes, chests of drawers, your grandmother's old trunk, or any other objects that could hinder qi movement.

If all your endeavors are in absolute stagnation, you should recheck the sector of the Traveling Horse. If you want changes and movement to come into your life, clear the space in these sectors, and your wishes will be carried out faster and easier. To speed them up, you need to activate these sectors in a specially selected day and hour.

What else can you use the Traveling Horse for? You can use it if you want to speed up anything; it is really helpful to speed up all the processes. If your Feng Shui is bad, you'll speed up a catastrophe, but if your Feng Shui is good, you'll speed up success. If you want to move somewhere, if you cannot get a visa—using the Traveling Horse star is a very good method for clearing obstacles. It can be used alone, because it is not linked with the Stars of the entrance door on the map or anything else.

FLYING STARS

Each of the flying stars represents a different thing. There is what you might call an official version, in which some stars are a big no-no, absolutely taboo, and some stars are good, which presents a rather "black and white" version of flying stars. In this school of thought, good stars, generally speaking, are one, six, and eight, which are the so-called White stars. There are natal maps of flying stars. There are stars associated with dates of things like construction; if your house was built in a certain year, we can calculate from that date and year and give you an appropriate flying stars map. This is an *esthetic version* of flying stars, but there is alternately a *dynamic version* of flying stars. With this dynamic approach, we are talking about annual stars and monthly stars and even daily flying stars.

For instance, in 2015, good star number 8 is located in the north, star number 1 is located in the southwest, and star number 6 is located on the northeast. Those sectors are good to spend time in and propitious places to locate your main door or your home office, etc.

The star number 8 brings you more opportunity for wealth, but generally speaking, it brings more opportunity for wealth if you work for somebody else. It's not such a good star for business owners. It creates more work, you are busier, and you have more money. But you cannot quadruple your money, for instance, with a star 8. You can however expect to gain 10 percent or 20 percent a year.

STUDENT SUCCESS STORY: I simply call him a magician!

"I learned about Feng Shui from Vladimir and how to do activations to stimulate wealth. This month I've done a lot of activations, both in the office and at home. When we prepared the report for September we found out that we earned an enormously greater amount compared to August. Our office had been open for a year without showing a profit during that time. We could barely pay our expenses. This month we finally hit the profit goal that our president had hoped for when he started the office. My coworkers were very skeptical at first. But we made an activation, and within an hour after this the head of a major bank came and ordered seals and stamps (this man had formerly been our client, but we had lost him to a competitor). At that point, my coworkers started to take it more seriously.

My coworker Larisa was the most skeptical. But one morning I came to the office, and it was very cold in the room, so I turned on a heater. And Larisa said,

'Anna, why are you doing this, there's nothing to activate today!'

'I'm just cold, Larisa!'

Curious, I checked the activations list, and she was right; there were no activations that day.

This meant that she studied this list when I was out! Last month my schedule kept me from making a number of activations at the proper times, because I was either in our house in the country or running from one office to another. But I still managed to make some activations. I worked for two offices, and I didn't even dream I'd get anything out of this personally as I know how our bosses "love" to pay their employees. But come payday I got an envelope with money. I counted it, but either it was a different sum than usual, or I couldn't add 2 to 3. I thought that I was just tired. When I recalculated it at home, I found out that I'd been given a bonus of $80! Now I'm looking forward to seeing next month's salary."

• •

Let's say, in a certain year when star number 8 is located on the south, you spend more room in your south room, or you have different doors inside of your house, and one of them is located in the south sector. If you use the south sector and you are an employee, it's not so bad. You'll have some kind of promotion or salary increase.

But for me, as a business owner, I would rather follow different stars, like star number 9. Star number 9 is good for joint ventures, and it is good for venture capitalists. It is good for businesses related to import and export or if you have business with foreigners and foreign companies. If you are going to expand your business and open branches in different cities, or even in different countries, star number 9 is very helpful.

You remember the story about Tom Sawyer who was told to whitewash a fence as punishment. He managed to make his friends believe he was actually enjoying the job, and they were so eager to try it that they traded their valuables to him just for the privilege of painting a small section while he lounged around and watched them. His Aunt Polly had ordered him to paint the fence, but he was clever enough to use this penalty as an opportunity to earn a little capital. That's what I'd call star 9 thinking: to see each crisis as an opportunity and somehow use it. It's been said that, "One person's tragedy is someone else's opportunity." That is star number 9.

Another good example is an enterprising postcard manufacturer that created postcards and sold them to American soldiers stationed in Iraq or Afghanistan, who sent them home to their families. The war was a disaster, but those guys made millions. That may strike you as cynical, but actually it's number 9 thinking.

Star number 6 is good for doing business with officials and governmental officers, with huge corporations, or with the military or police, corporations in which everything is organized and has a certain hierarchy. This is represented by star number 6. Star number 6 is about control.

Let's say you have a company and in a certain year, star number 6 flies in through your main door. It was west in 2014; it is northeast in 2015. In this year you have an opportunity to make good money with governmental contracts or with governmental institutions.

Perhaps you have a publishing company, and there is an election in your country. The government will need to order a lot of printed materials to support their election, and your company could make a killing. Star number 6 is about things like that.

Star number 1 is also a good star, one that's related to certain kinds of largely intellectual opportunities. If you're a student, you'll study and learn well. If you have a business related to water, it is especially good, whether you're running a bar or just selling water to fill swimming pools or even if you have an aquarium business. Also, if you have a logistic company, a transport-related company, or a travel agency, this year is good for you if you're under the influence of star number 1.

Under this black-and-white approach, in Feng Shui, the rest of the stars aren't so good. In fact, they get blamed for causing all kinds of disasters. Star number 7 creates gossiping, rumors, and lawsuits. It also causes accidents that lead to wounds and bleeding; if you are under the influence of star number 7 this year, you could get a nasty cut. Needing surgery and a higher risk of car accidents are also tied to star 7.

Star number 5 is the worst of all the stars. It creates tragedies and fatal diseases like cancer or stroke. It creates disasters like tsunamis and earthquakes.

Star number 3 is about fighting. It's about lost youth as well. It's about thievery, about theft; someone can steal your stuff or can rob you. Number 3 is like a gangster but not like a gangster boss, just a low level thug: not an Al Capone but one of his minions.

Star number 4 is about Peach Blossom. Star number 4 is not really bad; it's more of a 50/50 proposition. It creates a lot of peach blossoms, which play out in your life via love triangles, romances, and so on. From the good side, it brings creativity, a very strong and clever mind. You can study well, and your concentration is improved.

You'll have good marks on your exams. It's an artistic, academic star. But if you're a writer, a poet, or an artist, you're kind of creative, and because of that, you're surrounded by this Peach Blossom energy. There are a lot of people of the opposite sex who will be attracted to you, so you'll always have opportunities for romance. The problem is that if you're talking about singers and artists, they're quite often also surrounded by alcohol, drugs, and gambling—which is an example of this 50/50 thing. Think of it like the tail on a comet. There is the main part, which means academic knowledge and creativity, but also there is the tail of all kinds of bad things trailing behind.

Star number 2 is a star of diseases and doctors. You have a low energy level; you feel bad, you feel no energy, and sometimes your immune system doesn't work properly, so you'll be prey to different kinds of diseases. That's why number 2 is labeled the star of disease.

But actually, this white-and-black approach to these stars is not correct, because absolutes like black and white don't really exist in our lives. If you're a doctor and you have a star number 2 on your main door into your office, actually it's a good year for you because it brings you a lot of sick people. If there are no sick people, you have no business—so someone else's bad luck is your good fortune. If you're an owner of an antiques shop, star number 2 is good for you. And this star number 2 is also great for real estate; if you're a real estate dealer, your business is booming. If you're a real estate developer, your fortunes are influenced by star number 2, and this year is great for you. But as a sideways effect, you can develop a minor illness of some kind. Again, the energy is mixed.

Star number 5 is an Emperor Star, which makes it the strongest and most important of all the stars. If you look into a flying stars chart, this star number 5 is in the center.

It is called Luo Shu, after a character in a story, a Chinese tortoise that walked out the Luo River who had a particular pattern of dots on his shell. But to do well with it, you need to act like an emperor, to follow your own rules and not kiss anybody's butt. It helps to be the owner of a huge business. That's why star number 5 is bad for most people, because most people are slaves, not masters. To deal with this number 5, you need to be a master. You need to love your freedom more than your life. If you love freedom more than your life, star number 5 is perfect for you. But if you trade your freedom for money, for life, or whatever, this star number 5 actually will kill you. Start 5 is a huge money star, if you're the boss, a master, or an emperor. But if not, that sideways effect will get you.

Second-level money, but still potentially huge money, is star number 2, which means a lot of property, like at Donald Trump's level. But the sideways effect of this one is that you can become sick. Sure, you're a boss and wealthy, but you're also sick. You need to find a way to deal with the sickness part. If you have enough money, most sicknesses can be cured—but unfortunately not all of them.

The short level of money is the star number 8. This star is less risky than 5 and 2. But also, star number 8 creates less money than the others. There is a book I read recently that claimed that if you collect your wealth and spend less and earn a little bit more every year, you'll be a millionaire in 20 years. Those kinds of things are influenced by star number 8.

You can play your risks and rewards. The less risks involved in something, the less reward you have in the end, generally speaking. If you want to become wealthy really fast, you can use star number 5, but it's the most dangerous one. If you have more time, you can use star number 2, but the sideways effect is sickness; not necessarily always but quite often. If you're young, and you don't like risk, you can use star number 8 so that slowly over a period of years, but with no risk, you can become wealthy. Personally, I don't really have the patience, so I like star number 5.

Also, in talking about those stars, it's important to remember that they have interactions with your own star. If for instance you were born in 1979, or 1971, your personal star is star number 3 (register for free and put your date of birth into the Ba Zi calculator ba-zi.com). Star number 3 stands for revolutionary or rebellious people. And star number 5 is an emperor. An emperor is afraid of nothing but a revolution. So if you're star number 3, you'll find that star number 5 people are afraid of you. If your own star is number 3, you have certain advantages. You can fight against five and have huge money opportunities. It is still risky, but you can use certain Feng Shui techniques to lessen this risk and create a huge windfall or great opportunities for yourself. If it's not your own star, but it's inside of your house, it gives you the opportunity to take money—legally, of course!—from others. For instance, you can use aggressive marketing and rob your competitors of their customers. This star is perfect for all kinds of competitors, including athletes.

Star number 7 is not only best in terms of legal things, but it's also good for lecturers, teachers, and public speakers—anyone who earns their money with public talks. Also it's great for metaphysics, like Feng Shui, Western astrology, tarot, and so on. If star number 7 flies into your front door or into your bedroom this year and you started to learn metaphysics, or take up public speaking, you'll do very well. Also, if you're cut, either by accident or in surgery, you'll heal quickly and well. If you have legal problems, they'll come out to your advantage. The energy of this star goes to this metaphysics channel.

You can juggle these flying stars and choose whatever result you wish, either bad or good. That's a far more useful approach than the white-and-black approach so common in Feng Shui. If a bad star flies into my bedroom, then what? What can I do about it? Well, I'd need to sleep in another room. But if that room is also occupied by a bad star, then what? If that's the case, this kind of Feng Shui knowledge is not useful at all.

Quite often, Feng Shui isn't about changing your bedroom, or your main door; it's about changing your approach. You see your opportunities; you see your strength and weakness, so you proceed with your strengths and not your weaknesses. That's how you can change the aspect of a star from good to bad and from negative to positive.

It isn't just something you learn from reading a book. It takes years of study, and that is why a consultant is important. A consultant can guide you about the stars and their effects.

CHAPTER SIX

··

Feng Shui at the Office

In talking with business people who are interested in Feng Shui, I find there's a lot of misunderstanding of how to apply its principles correctly in a business environment. People try to take the same rules they've learned from Feng Shui for private houses and apartments and apply them to offices. It doesn't work. Worse than that, it can even be dangerous. Why? For private properties—homes and apartments—we're chiefly concerned with bringing harmony and happiness and relaxation. But for offices, if you and your employees are *too* happy and relaxed, chances are your company's going to go bankrupt. That's why we cannot use the same harmony principles for offices that we do for homes, because the business world is more like a war room environment.

When working with a business environment, our focus is results and bringing in profit. If you have to fire some employees on your way to accomplishing that, it's not a tragedy (unless you're consistently attracting bad employees). A business environment is more aggressive, so our Feng Shui principles are quite different and quite aggressive. Most Feng Shui consultants have never dealt with businesses and don't understand even the most fundamental principles. That's why I feel that it's very dangerous to your business to use them as Feng Shui consultants, because they're completely out of the business environment. Rather, choose a consultant who has a successful business and who understands how that environment differs from that of a home.

You can be a great Feng Shui master in the field of private life, or you can use Feng Shui principles to help a couple to conceive and have tremendous success. But if you're claiming to be a Feng Shui master and your own business is poorly run and unsuccessful, what does that say about your understanding of how to properly consult for others on business? It's like being fat and calling yourself a fitness trainer. I don't know why people can't see this when they're hiring an adviser; they'll choose unsuccessful Feng Shui masters who drive a very old car or use public transportation to reach their clients' houses, for instance. It's weird to me. What does that say about their success?

Business people tend to put a lot of emphasis on their management or their marketing, but they don't pay enough attention to their environment. Start with assessing simple things; perhaps you might realize if you observe yourself carefully that you are not very productive at your desk. For some reason, you're just not creative and energetic when you sit there. For me, I've found that I am quite productive sitting with my laptop in a restaurant or at the bar on the beach. The most productive place of all to work for me is an airplane; I find that when I'm flying I actually get four to five times more work done than I accomplish in any other environment. I don't know why that's the case, but clearly it's connected to Feng Shui, if you think of Feng Shui as an environmental study. **Even without technical Feng Shui knowledge, you can observe your environment and its influence on your productivity.** Again, Feng Shui is just a systematization of observations done during many centuries, so using it in business is a question of considering where your office or your place of business is located according to those systematic observations.

YIN AND YANG THEORY OF BUSINESS

Some locations are ideal for some sorts of businesses, and some are not. In assessing them, we can use Yin and Yang theory. Some businesses are Yin, while other businesses are Yang. Yin businesses are those in which you don't go to people but rather people come to you. You don't need as many clients as other businesses need. An example of Yin business would be a jewelry store. A store like that needs to sell one expensive piece of jewelry per month in order to be profitable.

The Yin businesses, like a jewelry store, can be in a quiet area; in fact, ideally, a Yin business should not be visible from the main street. In a Yin business, people either call you and make an appointment to visit your store, or you just take your goods with you and visit your client's house to show them. A Yin business should be a very VIP place where rich people come, so it needs to be located in an upscale area.

The Yang business, on the other hand, should be a crowded place like a main street where it will get a lot of foot traffic from passers-by.

There are some Yang businesses that need a lot of clients in order to turn a profit, for example supermarkets. Those businesses need to be in busy areas.

It's also important that the Yin and Yang inside and outside of an office or a shop should be balanced. Let me explain with some examples. Let's say you've got a bank that is located on an open, crowded public square, and outside it's typically very sunny and very bright. Most big banks, like Bank of America or Citibank, are Yang, and they require many clients, so they are generally located in very busy areas. But if your client comes in from the bright outdoors, and it's very Yin inside—by which I mean dimly lit, with low ceilings and dark colors—it's not balanced. This office space should mirror the Yang environment outside: light, bright, with high ceilings, and a feeling of air and spaciousness.

Normally, in Feng Shui, one of the nine principles is called Pure Yin, Pure Yang, which means that if the outside is Yin, the inside should be also Yin. If the outside is Yang, the inside should be also Yang. If your business is Yin, then your office should be Yin. If you've got a dark office with lots of black and gold décor, you'd better be selling coffins or funeral services.

That said, there are examples of places that need to be dark, because their businesses are moonlight inside, not sunlight, because the moon is Yin, a part of the night sky. Sun is Yang, in that it appears during the daytime. In a restaurant, I expect to see a kind of moon-like interior design with candles and everything, but sometimes there's very bright light or bright white tablecloths, and that creates a sense of disconnection. I've found that some clients, even if they have no idea about this Yin and Yang concept, are aware of that disconnect on an unconsciousness level. They look into a place and decide not to go in, because it just doesn't feel right.

Those bright places are normally empty at night. There are some exceptions; this can be changed by adjusting floor or ceiling levels and through mainly open at night. Bars and pubs and many restaurants need to have that kind of darker décor, with a cozy feeling, to be in line with the time of day that they do their business. When I take my girlfriend to a café for dinner, I don't want to see a lot of bright white lights. I want the feel of the concept of suppression of qi. But, generally speaking, those places don't do business after dark. The reverse is also true; those dark places are empty during the day, unless there is something dark outside. Let's say you're in an old city in Europe, in certain historic neighborhoods like those you find in Prague or Paris. There are small streets in the older areas, and the buildings there are close together. Those streets are normally dark, so if you open your shop or your café on one of those streets, it should be also dark, even during the daytime, so it's balanced. Then the business works. Otherwise, it will just sit empty, because nobody will want to come in.

....

STUDENT SUCCESS STORY: Mom calls me a fairy

A woman I knew had a six-month-old baby who suffered from respiratory problems and just wouldn't sleep through the night. Facing the bed in a new direction had a stunning effect: the baby stopped crying all night long, slept well, and lost all symptoms in two weeks' time. After that, his mom now calls me a fairy, but it has nothing to do with me; they were lucky it was such an easy one to fix."

But those are just the most rudimentary basics of the Yin and Yang concept. When I provide my consultations, I use much more profound approaches to it. Sometimes I'll suggest that your office door should be sunken, or sometimes that it should protrude. Sometimes, when you first enter, the space into which you walk should be small and then open up to be bigger. Sometimes it's vice versa. Generally, for Yin places, the space where you enter should be smaller, then widen out to a larger room. For Yang places, the entry area should be bigger, and then the subsequent space should be smaller. This is how we manipulate qi in order to fine-tune the qi inside of an office to the qi outside of an office.

The most important space for businesses like cafes or shops, apart from the location of the front door, is the location of the cashier. The cashier becomes the center point of the office's qi, because all money comes to this cashier's location. From the cashier's location, we track the Yin and Yang concept. Apart from this cashier, everything from the way out should be Yin, Yin, Yin, or Yang, Yang, Yang. As water flows out, qi flows out from the cashier, and from there, flows out from this business to the street. This arrangement practically guarantees that the business will be profitable. Again, we're using this alignment concept to create that domino effect. If it's out of alignment, and the flows are going in differing directions, then the qi becomes confused, the customers become confused, and the business doesn't do well. If the flow is good, the business will thrive.

I had a client whose business was suffering because of all kinds of issues he was experiencing with government regulators and difficulties in getting necessary certifications. He was running a travel business and had to be able to get the proper documents for his clients, but everywhere he seemed to be hitting walls and being told no. He had a lot of issues with consulates refusing to give visas for his clients. I looked at the Yin-Yang balance of his office and corrected it. First, I repositioned the door of his office and the table inside of his office. But, most importantly, I saw that there were steps from his office outside the main door. I just changed the angle of one step and solved the problem. How? I calculated in degrees to find controlling energy, the energy that means everybody wants to control you. By changing the angle of the step a little, I used the control against this control.

Within about six months, he had no more of those troublesome governmental issues. Those guys from the consulate not only gave him as many visas as he wanted but also now call him and ask him if he had more clients coming in, so that they can reserve more seats for him for the next month. His employees were quite shocked at this amazing turnaround.

PUTTING THE CART BEFORE THE HORSE

HOW MY CLIENT STEPPED ON A RAKE

Once a client invited me to make a Feng Shui audit of his new house. The house was almost complete and, as far as I understood, I just had to give some recommendations about the interior: bedroom, kitchen, office, entrance lobby, etc. When I asked about his reason for his interest in Feng Shui he told me the following story:

Numerous different problems had cropped up throughout the whole construction period. For example, roof metal tiles had to be replaced twice; the construction company had to be replaced. A mantelpiece also had to be remade twice for some reason. You can imagine the stress on the owner's nerves, not to mention material costs. But it was no wonder that the project was so challenging, as the house was being built in 2008 with a 0-degree north facing.

Keep in mind that construction had almost been finished when I was invited, that is the client had ordered a consultation post factum. A 0-degree facing refers to the Line of Death and Emptiness, plus in 2008 on the back of the house were located so-called afflictions or misfortunes: Three Sha, Year Duke, and Year Breaker. (These are terms of Feng Shui to reference certain energy patterns that change every year.) Thus, it was absolutely prohibited to start construction of a house with such a facing in 2008.

WHAT CAN BE DONE?

I suggested replacing the door to change the house orientation. But it was before the New Year, and the builders who lived out of town had already gone home for a couple of weeks to improve their liver conditions. The client said: "Okay, we'll change the door direction and all these things after they return."

However, while the builders were absent, the house sagged. There were only two possible scenarios. One was bracing it with steel cables, which would have spoiled the design. The other was taking it down and starting from scratch. So much for this guy's dream house.

I find it strange that people don't direct their effectiveness at problem prevention but wait until they create problems that they then have to struggle to solve. Wouldn't it be wiser to order a Feng Shui consultation first, *before* you start building?

The usual argument is that consultations are expensive. Is reconstructing a new house cheaper? What's the point of building a house, then having to remake the project or reconsider your sequence of actions? Do we buy materials before starting construction or vice versa?

Your house project should start with a consultation that takes in land selection, recommendations on the design, placement of doors, bedroom shapes, the best date for construction to start, house positioning according to cardinal directions, and door installation, all the way through to your best possible date to move in. This is the kind of work a Feng Shui consultant should do well before an architect takes up a pencil or opens a computer design program.

If we're talking about purchasing a condo or co-op, you need to consult before you choose an area, a floor, or the apartment itself. We need to specify a bed location for every occupant and a place for your stove. We have to arrange our plan according to the location of the main door and choose some kind of strengthening in the flat. If you've already bought the place and moved in, a lot of things can be still done, of course. You can adjust a bed location and select dates and activation places for accomplishing some goals for a propitious outcome.

"WE WON'T CHANGE ANYTHING!"

Sometimes, potential clients call and say: "Listen, we bought a condo, made repairs, placed a bed, we've had a design renovation and bought all new furniture, and it is impossible to make any changes. Please, come and do a consultation, but we won't change anything."

In my opinion, it is more logical to invite a Feng Shui consultant first and then do repairs and decoration, right? Likewise, if you live in an apartment or a house, a lot can be done still, providing you are ready for changes—replacing a bed, or a stove, or installing a temporary stove at least. Additionally, in order to effect positive changes in your well-being, you must be ready to do these things at certain dates. If you want something in your life to change, you have to be open to making changes.

Our life is perfectly arranged to get the results we are getting. If we want to get different results, then life has to be redesigned and changes very likely made in our house, as we spend many hours there daily. If you consider Feng Shui first and then start renovation or construction, the result will be a good house that will bring you and your family bliss and well-being.

Unfortunately, very often people do repairs or start construction first and invite a Feng Shui consultant when everything is finished. Thus they put a cart before a horse and get a house that has to be taken apart. It can lead to a family break-up, loss of business, loss of income, or worse.

"BUT A FENG SHUI AUDIT IS SO EXPENSIVE!"

I agree: it is much "cheaper" to rebuild a house, to lose business or a job, or to suffer from serious diseases that disturb all the occupants of your house. And, of course, you'd better listen to your relatives: "One should be a sensible, grown-up person and should not waste money on such silliness." Then you'll be okay, like 99 percent of "sensible, grown-up, rational, smart people" around you—those who live on a hand-to-mouth salary or pension and have stopped dreaming and hoping for better lives.

Indeed, Feng Shui services are expensive, and you may not be able to afford a Feng Shui audit or take a professional course in Malaysia or Singapore. But there are some simple rules you can follow to make a basic audit on your own, not the in-depth kind that a professional can offer, of course, but for those of you making your first or early steps in Feng Shui. Check out my website; it will get you started.

WHY IS SOME REAL ESTATE HARD OR IMPOSSIBLE TO SELL?

And why is it that, even with the help of Feng Shui, activation of this real estate can be extremely difficult?

In Chinese metaphysics we talk about three types of luck: heaven luck, human luck, and earth luck. Only when these three types of luck unite—that is, when there is a house with a human in it, bringing with him his human qi—does Feng Shui appear. If a house is not inhabited, if no one lives there, it is not possible to activate anything in order to sell it via Feng Shui.

How can you bypass these restrictions?

Well, there are two ways to do this. The first one is quite specific and has to be done in a very particular way. It requires that you have to actually move into this house or put someone else into the home, let's say a builder. That will activate the human qi.

You need to select an auspicious date and do the usual ritual of settling in: come to the house, cook some meals and eat them there, have tea, etc., and spend a night or two. After this, when you or someone else settles there, you should stay through the next day and you shouldn't go out anywhere the day following that. Then, you should just come on a regular basis to this house, making sure that the period between your visits is no longer than 48 hours. If it is longer, then you've undone your work; it is as though this was the first time you came, and the new date is activated, rather than the auspicious one you chose before. That may have unpredictable effects.

A second, somewhat less-demanding way, is to carry out a special activation ritual. Again, you should select an auspicious date to come to this house or apartment you are going to sell. Once you're there, open all the windows, turn on the taps, turn on loud music, make plenty of noise, and burn incense sticks. While you do these things, you should be making wishes that this house or apartment will be sold quickly, to good people, at a price that is good for you, and wishing that its new inhabitants enjoy a favorable qi.

When we talk about the absence of human qi in uninhabited homes, this doesn't apply, naturally, to houses or apartments that people have already lived in or rented. You don't have to carry out an activation ritual in such houses or apartments. You just have to pick an auspicious date to activate qi, if this house or apartment has stood empty for a long time.

If you're trying to sell a piece of empty land, it is even more critical, as there are no buildings where you can activate qi. You cannot activate qi merely on a piece of soil. To sell it, you have to do some rituals in your own apartment or home that will activate human qi. You must select a date and make a Feng Shui formula that it is aimed at activation of selling this land at a good price.

Let's talk a little about the three primary components in the sale of real estate: psychology, the choice of the date, and the activation of Feng Shui.

When it comes to the choice of the date and hour, one of the best hours you can choose is the hour of the Traveling Horse. You can find it in the free online Ba Zi calculator, at www.ba-zi.com (the tab "Auspicious Dates"). If you click a certain hour, you'll see auspicious stars in green and inauspicious stars in red.

Hour	Day	Month	Year	
7	4	1	9	XKDG element
戊 Wu	丙 Bing	壬 Ren	甲 Jia	Heavenly stems
子 Zi	辰 Chen	申 Shen	午 Wu	Earthly branches
4	1	7	1	XKDG period

Hour Description
Heavenly Officer
Heavenly Prison
Group Emptiness

Energies of the Day
Direct clash
Hour/year
Bad for the Dog

9.Success

Auspicious for: The most auspicious day. Religious rituals, engagement, marriage, business, deals conclusion, travels, taking the post, visits, renovation, construction works, choosing a treatment method, funeral (good Yin Feng Shui and increase of descendants). Day that increases outcomes, thus it is good to use it for positive actions.
Inauspicious for: Lawsuits (there will be more if them!), demolition (dismantling)

28 Moon stands

Constellation: Basket

Day of week: Wednesday
Auspicious for: Construction works, collection of debts
Inauspicious for: Marriage, funeral

Among these stars you will find a Star of the Traveling Horse. It is not always available or may be available only in hours of clash or conflict. In other cases, you can choose the hour of the Traveling Horse. And it should be one of four Earth signs: Pig, Snake, Tiger, or Monkey. Nothing else. During these hours, you can place an ad about selling a piece of real estate; if you have placed it already, you can deactivate it for three days and then, within these hours, place it again for a much better result.

And now—setting the price. The price of an object is derived from the Chinese metaphysics method: it is either Xuan Kong (flying stars) or Xuan Kong Da Gua. We can take those numbers from the space or have a look at the map of flying stars or take your table of birth and find the so-called Xuan Kong Da Gua numbers. In any case, there should be some consistency that is reflected in the price. It doesn't have to be the final price, but this is the bid price, the one potential buyers see in the ad. Sometimes it can be unusual, such as $539,643.

People may call and ask: "Why do you have such an unusual price?"

And you answer: "Well, it *is* unusual, but you've called!"

In Feng Shui you can use the so-called "the Traveling Horse" sector inside of your home, in the entrance hall of your house or apartment, or according to the Big Tai Qi. It should be calculated in respect to the direction of the entrance hall of the apartment building, for an apartment, or in respect to the direction of the front door, for a house. Ideally, we should kill two birds with one stone, activating this sector in this specific day, hour, and location, using a toy car or a horse figure. You can also make some noise, burn a candle, etc.

What can you do if you do not know the Traveling Horse ritual? You can use the Four Good Guys method. For this, you should choose an hour of the Traveling Horse and activate one of the Good Guys.

Speaking of psychological methods for the apartment or house sale, you can do the following: before your client comes, you should either burn coffee-scented incense sticks or make real coffee. This method is well known to Realtors, and one woman who works as a Realtor in Singapore told me that she uses this method in combination with Feng Shui methods and that it does help her to successfully sell real estate.

What else can you do? You can bring a good-looking set of furniture you buy or lease from a furniture store and furnish your empty apartment or house before a client arrives so that it looks like someone lives here. This helps to show that this place is flourishing and successful and create a "wow" effect—a client will think, "I never imagined that such prosperous families lived here!" I also recommend clearing the house or apartment of any clutter, washing the windows, etc. All this usually creates a good impression.

We also use methods of pushing in and pushing out of qi; we use San He methods and methods of qi transformation. But these are more complex than can be explained in the context of this book, and a Feng Shui specialist is really required to come to the location and make measurements in order to apply them.

CHAPTER SEVEN:
Feng Shui in Family Life and Relationships

Feng Shui can help tremendously in the smooth running of family and love lives. Alternatively, a home with bad Feng Shui can hurt such interactions.

There are two main areas in which Feng Shui principles can help to create and maintain good personal relationships. First, if you currently don't have enough relationships in your life, Feng Shui can help you to have more. Also, if you want a stable relationship, Feng Shui can help, but that depends on the personal philosophy and approach of your Feng Shui master. For me, it's much easier to bring a new relationship or more and different partners to my clients than it is to help someone who wants to stabilize an unhappy relationship or to deal somehow with troubles in their current relationship. I find it easier to get a client out of his or her current relationship and into a new and better one, but it is possible to work with what you have.

PEACH BLOSSOM SECTOR

If my client is a woman who has no partner and wants one, there are several options. Of course, I could start my own relationship with her, but if I am currently working with her in the context of a client/ Feng Shui master relationship, that's not always ideal. Generally, we would work with the Peach Blossom sector, the sector for romantic relationships. There are tables available that will tell you where you fall in the Peach Blossom sector via your date of birth. Let's imagine I have a client, and she has a Peach Blossom sector of east 2. It's either east 2, middle of the east, middle of the west, middle sector of west, middle sector of south, or middle sector of north, but in this case let's say it's the east sector. Peach Blossom qi brings us new partners. But it also brings charm and charisma if you have this Peach Blossom energy—even if you're old and fat like me. You may not be what's generally considered handsome, or you know you're no beauty, yet somehow people are attracted to you. When you meet someone who has this energy, you experience a strong pull of attraction and a sense of being immediately connected. You meet a girl and you just fall for her at first sight. If your best friend asks you, you won't be able to explain logically why you love this girl. It wasn't anything special that she did or said, but somehow you like her. It's about Peach Blossom energy.

This energy should not be blocked inside of your house. Once you know where your Peach Blossom (romance) sector is, it should not have any oversized furniture in it.

Peach Blossom Table

Year/Day Branch			Peach Blossom
Shen Monkey	Zi Rat	Chen Dragon	You (Rooster)
Hai Pig	Mao Rabbit	Wei Goat	Zi (Rat)
Yin Tiger	Wu Horse	Xu Dog	Mao (Rabbit)
Si Snake	You Rooster	Chou Ox	Wu (Horse)

You could have a chair in there but not a huge table or a wardrobe. Also, no big flowerpots or planters should be in this sector. It's better to keep the sector clean and bright and open. If you do this, you'll quickly discover that people seem to suddenly like you a lot more—not only in terms of personal relationships but also in terms of business; somehow people trust you and they want to spend time with you. Thus, because you have more options and more opportunities, you'll always have somebody new to choose from and date.

Many people think that Peach Blossom is just about finding sex and extramarital affairs. They assume that if you are married it's better not to activate the sector because it brings a new partner into your life. Now, that doesn't have to be a problem at all (although it can become one if you're caught by your spouse. It's great for the lawyers, though; all those settlements and billable hours!) What I mean is that you're in no way compelled to use all those opportunities that will come at you. People will simply like you more and be more attracted to you. What you do about it is up to you. Depending on your personality, you can either have a great time with them without taking it to the bedroom level, or you can proceed with caution. If you're the kind who can't say no, and you're happy with your partner/spouse, you might be better off not activating the Peach Blossom energy, although it can also help you with business, as I've said, making people find you more appealing and trustworthy. But if you're a lonely person in search of a partner, you can find Feng Shui a lot more useful than those courses on how to pick people up. That first and big step is to open up that space and get rid of furniture blocking it. If you're resistant to that idea—if you're more attached to the furniture than you are to the idea of having a soul mate—then your resistance may tell us that you're not really interested in that kind of relationship, even if you think you are.

Let's say I discover that the Peach Blossom sector in my client's house is blocked by a wardrobe, so I tell my client it's better to move this wardrobe to the other corner. If he or she doesn't like that, then he or she has not much interest in a relationship. But sometimes they really respond badly to the suggestion, and I hear a lot of complaints like, "I cannot move this furniture. It's very expensive," or, "I have no other space for this furniture. That's the only corner it can be in." That to me is a sign of much bigger hidden issues and a sign they definitely need to remove this furniture to improve their relationship life.

Equally important is that you can't have a bathroom in your Peach Blossom sector, because then you're guaranteed shaky relationships if you get any at all. I had a client with this problem; she ended up with a married guy who kept promising he loved her and that he'd leave his wife for her but never did. That went on for seven years, and that's not the only story like that I've heard.

It's good to keep tabs on where your spouse's Peach Blossom sector is. Let's say there is a couple and the husband has his Peach Blossom sector activated somehow accidentally, maybe by the random placement of a fountain or aquarium in this sector or a huge vase. His wife had better be paying attention to her husband's love life if that happens, because that will be bringing him opportunities for new relationships.

STUDENT SUCCESS STORY: "You Never Know!"

"Before I learned about Feng Shui, I used to be a skeptical, down-to-earth woman who didn't trust in such things. Every-thing started when a friend of mine (who is easily carried away) suggested making calculations of my fate. I didn't really believe in horoscopes—but why not try it if it would make her happy? By the time I met with her the next time, all the calculations were ready. I got a piece of paper with a chart drawn by hand and some vague explanation that I didn't have enough water and fire, so I would never be rich or have a lot of happiness, etc. It's hard to recall the details now. As it turned out later, the calculations were incorrect. But it didn't really matter. It was the bad prognosis that made me react so strongly.

Searching for information, I began to buy and study special literature and surf the Internet; it was an exciting and stimu-lating process. First, I studied Ba Zi, then Gua numbers, then flying stars. I must say that, at that time, my life flew quite smoothly. My husband had a good job, we travelled often, and I didn't really plan any major changes in life. But, as we say, man proposes, but God disposes—and I started the most fascinating journey in my life. My interest in interior design got an additional support and an absolutely new meaning. Furniture found new locations I couldn't even have thought of before. Old clothes and things that we used to love found new owners and a second life.

My husband and I were surprised to find out that we could fall asleep more quickly and sleep well if the bed is in a good sector and in an auspicious direction. Our home became more peaceful and cozier. Our troubled neighbors gradually calmed down. At least we didn't get woken up at night from the loud sounds and music.

Miracles happened at my husband's office, too. He moved his desk so that it stood in an auspicious direction. Gradually, the situation at work got less tense. And his schedule was also changing for the better. He began to get back home from work much earlier. We'd got time for hobbies we could only dream of before. In our forties, we went in for swimming, having found a good coach and a swimming pool (a sports club had all of a sudden opened next door).

And there are many more such "little things"! They are not limited to just our family. After having practiced Feng Shui for a couple of years, I started helping loved ones a bit.

We rearranged furniture in my friend's apartment in accordance with her Kua number—and her daughter got into a university. Then, out of nowhere an old friend showed up and offered to pay her fees for her. The minor renovation and redecoration of another friend's office allowed her to finally breathe freely. As she said, she'd been like the hamster in *the spinning wheel for five years, without an opportunity to spend time with her children. Her desk is no longer placed between the window and the door; she faces one of her best directions, and her life no longer feels like a constant battle. She spends much more time with her children.*

And now, the most interesting thing: A few years ago my husband and I wanted to emigrate to another country. We had made several attempts, but every time something was stopping us: a new and interesting job, graduation from the university, my mom's illness. After trying and failing several times, we thought it was not meant to happen and stopped trying. But after two years work with the internal and external space, we got a chance to buy an apartment in a European country (I wouldn't have believed it two years ago!). We jumped on it. Moreover, it opened up other opportunities. Now, we're learning a foreign language, we've got new wonderful friends, and we have a chance to start our business. We live in two cities, two countries now, but we love traveling, so this is great.

Needless to say that life does not always go smoothly, no matter how hard you try. But I can say for sure that Feng Shui helps to smooth out the bumps and helped us to weather the storms better. In any case, for me Feng Shui is not just a tool for changing the space around me and improving life situations. Feng Shui gives me an opportunity to study the world around and, what is even more important, to learn about myself and my place in the world. I wish everyone success in studying and implementing Feng Shui."

It's a good idea if you're getting serious about someone to consult Chinese astrology with your birth information and theirs. It can take years to understand this stuff, but generally speaking, you'll be talking about the same Peach Blossom star, not inside of your house but inside of your astrology: your battery chart and your four pillars chart. If you have this Peach Blossom star inside of your astrology chart, then you are more attractive and more people like you. The star can be inside or outside; if it's in your annual pillar or your month pillar then it's outer Peach Blossom star. But if it's in your day pillar or hour pillar, then it's your internal Peach Blossom star, so it can be either external or internal. If it's external, then you show this Peach Blossom energy outside of your house. If it's internal, then you show your Peach Blossom energy to your husband or wife or to somebody inside of your house.

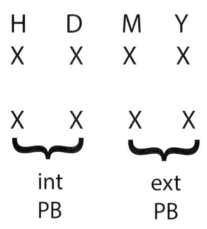

Let's say I meet a woman, and she has one Peach Blossom star. I might assume that it's advisable to marry her if it's internal, like day pillar or hour pillar, because I'd think that meant that she shows her beauty to me only, not to everybody. But the problem is that even if she shows her beauty only inside of your house, that might mean she'd also be attractive to the pool guy or the gardener. If I've got a good-looking guy painting my living room, and my wife is bored—well, you can see how that could play out. So just choosing someone on the basis of that would be dumb.

In old times, the rich and powerful used Chinese astrology to check the qualities of potential wives and paid attention to the patterns in their charts in assessing them. There's one pattern they avoided, and you should, too. It's an argumentative pattern; if I say something's black, she'll insist it's white. If I switch and agree with her—right, it's white—she'll tell me it's black. That means there will always be strife in the home. The name of this pattern translates loosely into "Hurting Officer Structure." It means to disagree too much with what her husband and boss say. Now that divorce is legal, it's not as bad as it was in former days when you were stuck together for life, but even so, a woman with this pattern should not be a housewife. She needs to have a job, because then she kills her boss instead of you.

Take a woman who has a lot of Peach Blossom energy inside of her chart. There always will be competition for her. You always will need to show you're a better husband, a better lover, a better whatever than those other guys. You'll have your hands full trying to control her, and you're likely to lose her in any case, because there is always somebody wealthier and younger, or at least newer than you are, so probably she'll disappear anyway. I wouldn't choose a woman like that for a long-term relationship, although for a short-term relationship she'd be just fine.

Not everything is run by Peach Blossom stars, of course; there's a lot more to relationships and Feng Shui than that. For example, there is star number 4. This star also brings Peach Blossom luck, and it changes its position every year; for instance, in 2015 it's northwest in the southern, in 2016 it's the west, and so on. And if you spend a lot of time in a room occupied by this star, you will also have this Peach Blossom energy.

Many years ago I had a client who was lonely and complaining that she had no boyfriend. She had a great career but nobody to love; she was actually quite a high-ranking executive, which probably cut into the time she had for dating. When I checked her apartment I found that there was a huge flowerpot inside of her Peach Blossom sector, and I advised her to remove this pot immediately. Also, the energy in the bedroom she slept in was not good. I discovered that there was this number 4 Peach Blossom star in the room she was using as a family room, so I advised her to sleep in her family room instead of her bedroom. She didn't like that idea and told me that it wasn't convenient because she had a nice bed in her bedroom but just the sofa in her family room, and on and on. But I convinced her. I told her there was no obligation to sleep your whole life in this family room; just try it for one or two months, maximum. If it works, it works. If it doesn't work, it doesn't. In my experience, that's as long as it should ever take for good Feng Shui to show itself. Sometimes it's several hours, sometimes it's several weeks, but there's no reason to wait a few years for results to appear. If it just appears, it appears; that's fine. She agreed, so I found a good day for her to move into her family room, and she started sleeping in there.

Two months later I was meeting with her sister, who is also my client, and she told me then her sister had gotten married just one month before. So, in one month after this consultation she was not only dating but was married—whoa! Frankly, I thought that was a little *too* quick; I mean it takes some time to get to know each other, right? Especially since I knew she was a smart and accomplished woman, not some brainless lovesick teenager. I was kind of shocked, but later on I found out that she was married to her former college friend, so they'd known each other before. They hadn't seen each other for years—he'd been married, then divorced—and they'd reconnected with a happy ending. Because he was leaving for another country, they had to marry quickly, because of visa issues that would have kept her from joining him for a long time. She wound up moving with him and leaving that apartment to her sister. I ended up consulting on that same apartment but for a different person, the sister. There was only one case I consulted the same property for two different people, but it was interesting. And guess why? Her sister was having the same kinds of issues! She was dating a married man, and she was looking for a real relationship that could lead to marriage.

I also fixed this apartment for her but in a different way than I had for her sister. I repositioned her bed, just using a different angle. She found a permanent boyfriend, and they got married. When they started to build a new house, I also consulted those house planners and advised her on the best move-in date and everything else related to that project. Then when she became pregnant, I found the best date for caesarian surgery, I gave them some advice for the newborn child, and then I gave them some advice for their business. I didn't see them for years, then they invited me to this new house with big trees grown up all around it, and their little girl was 12 years old already. Last time I'd seen that place, it was empty, and their baby was just two months old. I hadn't felt that 12 years pass until I saw how the trees and the daughter had grown. Stuff like that that makes you feel old!

HEALTH ISSUES

Bed placement can affect more than your love life, by the way. Once I assisted my master. He was consulting with a governmental official of Malaysia. And this guy had had a stroke, and he couldn't speak and couldn't walk without help. We checked his bedroom, and it was not okay at all. There was a better bedroom on the second floor, but because he could not walk, it was not an option because he needed to use the staircase to walk up and down. To solve the problem, we used an old Yang Gon Feng Shui technique, which can be tracked to Grand Master Yang Yun Sun, from the ninth century. The origins of most Feng Shui schools can be tracked to this Grand Master. Another student and I helped my master to do the measurements and calculations. We repositioned the bed of this client into a precise direction and a precise angle in order to bring health energies to it. In this calculation we used the bed direction and the quality of qi that came from the door into his room. There are twelve stages of qi, and we used one of them to bring some health luck.

The results came very quickly. In a couple of weeks he started to talk a little bit and to walk a little bit, and a couple months later he'd improved even more. His doctors had told him that he'd probably never talk or walk again; he didn't regain complete freedom of motion or great diction, but he was talking and walking.

What I want to illustrate is that Feng Shui works even for such severe cases, and it definitely can help even more for health issues where there is less damage, because many cancers can be tracked back to Feng Shui. How? As you probably are aware, there is water moving through the Earth in underground springs. Some people's homes are on top of these springs, whether or not they're aware of them. The water is sometimes diverted into a culvert or pipe under the house, which creates a huge cut in the qi under that house. If you position your bed above this underground stream, then there is a huge chance in a few years you'll have severe health issues: maybe cancer, or stroke, or a heart attack. It can also lead to a car accident. That's why it's vitally important to check the energy quality inside of your house and inside of your bedroom and improve this qi quality as much as possible. While I know that many people think primarily of Feng Shui as a way to bring them more material wealth, there's nothing more important than health, and Feng Shui is a powerful tool with which to create and preserve your good health. After all, if you are dead, money won't be of much use to you. As Steve Jobs said, "Being the *richest* man in the cemetery doesn't matter to me."

CONCEPTION ISSUES

Many people come to me to consult on fertility issues. At my website www.ba-zi.com/theconceptionsector, you'll find a link to a calculator that will help you to locate your conception sector (of course for women only). If there is something moveable in this conception sector, then a woman cannot get pregnant, or she may lose the child. Even if a couple uses *in vitro* fertilization, they won't succeed; because there's something moving inside of her womb, this conception sector is not stable, lowering their chances of success-ful conception and pregnancy. Fortunately, there's a lot we can do to fix the problems using Feng Shui, and many of my clients are parents now because they followed the advice they got through their consultation.

For instance, if you use the best dates for *in vitro* fertilization, or even for marriage, it can help a lot. That said, it can't work miracles; if you and your spouse to be are a bad match on a deeper level, it won't matter what date you choose, because you'll be miserable anyhow. But why not maximize your chances for a smooth life together by choosing the most propitious date? Even if you ultimately do separate, having made those kinds of choices from the start may mean that your separation goes more easily and with less drama. Think of it like having a strong immune system. Even if you have one, you're bound to get sick sometimes. But you'll get less ill and bounce back more quickly than a person whose immune system is weak.

Into every life some rain must fall. Feng Shui helps you avoid those storms, but it doesn't promise you'll never get wet.

IN CLOSING...

I hope I've given you a better understanding of the potential and power available to you through an understanding and application of the principles of Feng Shui. It's important to realize that it's about more than just rearranging furniture; it's about all the small and big decisions we make. There is an energy structure in our bodies, in our houses, and in our offices. By being aware of and channeling the energy of the stars in certain days and hours, we may only need to do small things—but these small things bring huge change in our lives. Those who don't understand Feng Shui may think it's a lot of work, that you have to make tremendous changes, and that you're required to upend your whole house and its arrangement or to radically transform your behavior and so forth. But that's not the case. I'd advise you instead to change something small, because when you do so, the whole system changes automatically. It's like when we are driving a car: there are signs we have to watch and other cars nearby, and the outlook is constantly in motion. You can't get to where you want to go by doing nothing; you have to make a million tiny adjustments every minute to keep your car going in the right direction toward your goal and to avoid hazards. But it doesn't feel that way to an experienced driver; all this stuff just comes automatically. It's totally doable and within our ability. Each step is accomplished seamlessly, and one follows another. It simply takes training and experience.

What many people tend to do is to overcomplicate simple things. I'd suggest, rather, that you try some of the techniques and approaches described in this book and see your results. If you'd like more support and more information, or if you'd like to see some videos I've made that might make it all more clear for you, you can go to my website, www.vladimirzakharov.com/fsnewsletter, and subscribe to my free newsletter. And don't hesitate to get in touch if you have questions. I can help you to understand whatever is unclear to you in this book or in Chinese metaphysics in general.

If you're still wondering whether it's worth trying, let me explain my point of view this way. Say that we are in the middle of a dark room; we have no light to guide us, but somehow we need to find our way out. We can stand there and do nothing; that's an option, although it won't get us anywhere until the sun comes up. But if we're willing to risk taking a first step, then we'll get a little feedback from the space around us. Maybe we'll discover that we can touch a wall, or we come into contact with a piece of furniture that we can feel our way around. Sooner or later, we'll find the wall, and we can follow it to a door or a window. Finally, we can unlock this door or window and get out of the dark room and into the light. But the person who just stands in the dark, thinking and worrying and making predictions about what may happen, will never win using that approach. If you want something to change, you have to make a change.

We can take the metaphysical approach that everything is related to everything and everybody exists in relation to everyone else. Everything impacts everything. If we change the people around us, our space will change. If we change the space around us, the people around us will change too. If we can learn to use this interconnection law via some simple techniques, we will finally see results that will give us more trust in this holistic approach. We will have more trust in this cause-and-effect approach, which tells us that we create our own future and our present condition is created by our actions in the past and the current moment we create.

In fact, we are in the process of constructing our future right now. Chinese metaphysics gives us the language to describe this cause-and-effect interconnection, but regardless of whether or not you describe it with Chinese terminology, these things are just reality. It's not like a belief system; it is as concrete and immutable as the laws of physics. Regardless of whether or not you believe in gravity, the glass of water you drop will fall down, not fly up. Your belief system has no bearing on this fact. That's true of the laws of metaphysics, too. Why not use them to your advantage, rather than having them work against you—or trying to work against them? That's what Feng Shui will help you with, and by doing so, make your life run that much more smoothly and successfully on all levels.

Nine Ways to Improve Your Life Right Now

If you take nothing else from this book, I'd like you to do the things I've listed below as first steps. I promise you, they will change the way you look at Feng Shui.

1. **Location Test #1; Rich people live in areas for the rich, and poor people live in areas for the poor.**

   Obviously, there are some exceptions. But there are no tips for interior Feng Shui that can make these exceptions a rule. What should you do to improve the situation? Move from the area of depression into the area of progress.

   If you cannot afford to do it right now, look for an interim situation that's at least a step up.

2. Location Test #2

The area you live or work in is not considered good if you have to overcome barriers to get to and from it—like driving long distances, getting through daily traffic jams, or having to travel along bad or narrow roads. This is especially true for offices. If any of these barriers stand between you and your home on a regular basis, change your home or workplace.

3. Look out of the window of your room.

Are there any sources of Sha qi (a transmission tower, the smokestack of a factory, a cemetery, a tank on a pediment, or a building site) within view? If the answer is yes, do not make this room a bedroom, for heaven's sake! And do not activate this sector with a candle or a fountain.

4. Make your home a home of a rich person.

If you think that in order to accomplish this, you need to upgrade everything immediately—do a renovation, buy designer furniture, or get a place with an ocean view—you are wrong!

Define one thing that evokes in you a feeling of being rich—and buy that thing.

For me, that feeling is evoked by having a brand new Mac laptop in an almost-empty room. I don't care if it has plain brick walls and a mattress for sleeping on the floor.

The next most important thing to me is having a great view from the window of the upper floor.

You need to find your own way to wealth and make sure that that one meaningful, evocative object is there in your room and in your sight.

And please—not some junky kitsch from Chinese flea markets! No cheap toads, no Hotei, no Chinese coins!

5. Select auspicious dates for important events.

Every time you start a project, apply for a job, sign a contract, or schedule a wedding, make sure you've chosen the most auspicious date. Doing this, you can easily multiply your income several fold.

6. Buy yourself the best mattress you can find.

Yes, a mattress! It is just amazing: people spend so much money buying things that gather dust in their closets and go out of date in a few months but disregard the mattress where they spend eight hours a day, 240 hours a month, and 2,920 hours a year. With a proper mattress, you'll get a first-class rest, a healthy back, and a trigger of wealth.

And in case you think my advice on mattresses isn't worth much, I'll add that I learned about this from Michael Masterson, one of the most progressive minds in today's business world.

7. The impact of the environment.

It is impossible to think about great things in a miserable milieu. Go to a hotel lounge or bar with a great interior or to a restaurant with a wonderful city view, order a cup of coffee at least, and picture your splendid and bright life in your head.

Social surroundings also matter! As one guru of personal growth once said: "The things I teach you won't work if you are surrounded by shallow people who drag you down with their doubts, envy, and disbelief". If they are telling you: "*You* can't do this," they are actually saying, "*I* can't do this."

If you put a crab into a basket, he will climb out. But if you put two crabs into a basket, you don't have to worry, as they will be dragging each other down and no one will escape.

8. The mountain and the water

Be sure mountain and water can be seen from your property. Either one, or even better, both. Position your bedroom on the side of the mountain provided it's a good-looking mountain or hill. If neither is visible, 80 percent chance the place has low-quality Feng Shui, so please find some suggestions in my article fengshuimillionaire. com/10th-house.

9. Which of my clients and students make me really proud?

Those who not only study Feng Shui but also use it in their everyday lives.

Knowledge is power, but this is true only if you use it. Otherwise, libraries would be the most powerful places on Earth.

I wish you the best Feng Shui.

Vladimir Zakharov

.